Transform!

Transform!

How everyday things are made

Written by Bill Slavin with Jim Slavin

Illustrated by Bill Slavin

OXFORD

UNIVERSITY PRESS

OXFORD
UNIVERSITY PRESS

Great Clarendon Street, Oxford OX2 6DP
Oxford University Press is a department of the University of Oxford.

It furthers the University's objective of excellence in research,
scholarship, and education by publishing worldwide in

Oxford   New York

Auckland   Cape Town   Dar es Salaam   Hong Kong   Karachi
Kuala Lumpur   Madrid   Melbourne   Mexico City   Nairobi
New Delhi   Shanghai   Taipei   Toronto

With offices in

Argentina   Austria   Brazil   Chile   Czech Republic   France   Greece
Guatemala   Hungary   Italy   Japan   Poland   Portugal   Singapore
South Korea   Switzerland   Thailand   Turkey   Ukraine   Vietnam

Oxford is a registered trade mark of Oxford University Press
in the UK and in certain other countries

Text © Bill Slavin with Jim Slavin 2005

Illustrations © Bill Slavin 2005

The moral rights of the author have been asserted

Database right Oxford University Press (maker)

First published in 2005 by Kids Can Press Ltd.
29 Birch Avenue, Toronto, ON, Canada M4V 1E2

Published in the UK by Oxford University Press 2006

Edited by Valerie Wyatt and Kathy Vanderlinden
Designed by Esperança Melo and Marie Bartholomew
Anglicization of text by Ben Dupré

British Library Cataloguing in Publication Data

Data available

ISBN-13: 978-0-19-911504-4
ISBN-10: 0-19-911504-4

10 9 8 7 6 5 4 3 2 1

Printed in China

Kids Can Press is a **ℓ℮ℕ℺** Entertainment company

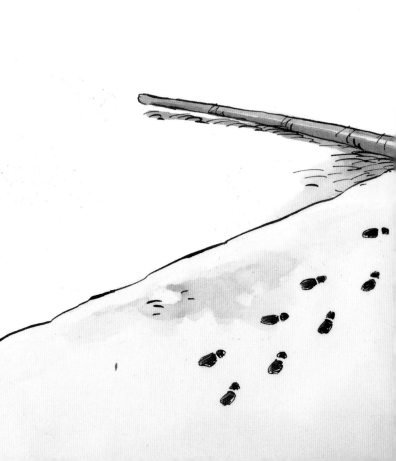

About This Book

This book was designed and typeset on a state-of-the-art computer. The artwork was scanned and colour-separated using a computer-run scanner. The pages were printed on a giant printing press that can print hundreds of pages in the blink of an eye! Other machines sorted the pages and bound them into books …

If you stepped inside a modern factory, all you'd be likely to see is loads of big, computer-operated machines whirring away and mysteriously turning out finished products at the end. When I started working on this book, I wondered how I was going to show what was really going on. But I soon realized that in spite of the complex technology, the basic steps objects go through as they are changed from raw materials into finished products have stayed essentially the same over the years. So I decided to concentrate on showing those steps.

I also chose common items we are all familiar with – mass-produced trainers instead of custom-made dress shoes, and factory-made bread rather than the home-baked variety. Where the action of a machine seemed necessary to the creation of an object, I tried to show that action. But I spent less time explaining the many kinds of ovens and mixers needed to make almost everything here.

The final chapter, Back to Basics, is the key to the book, since it deals with the raw materials used to make many of the simple objects you will find in these pages. I hope that most of the time you will be able to follow an object's transformation from animal, vegetable or mineral all the way to its final form.

As for the artwork for this book, it was produced on a wooden drawing table, on paper made from cotton, using watercolours and a quill inking pen – all technologies developed hundreds of years ago.

Bill Slavin

Contents

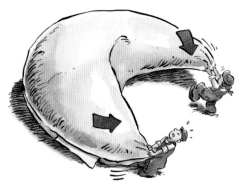

Introduction

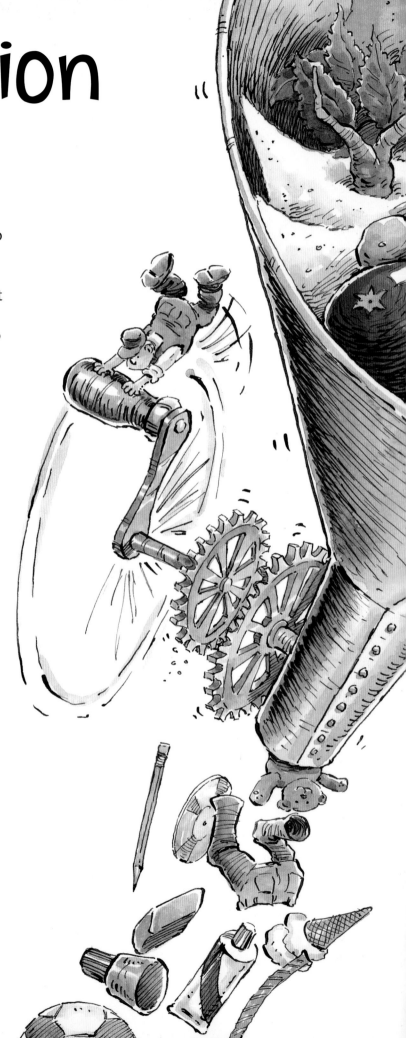

You live in a world of mysteries, surrounded in your daily life by things you know very little about.

Take an ordinary day. In the morning you jump into a pair of jeans. (How were they made, and why are they blue?) At school, you and your friends kick around a football. (How did it get that perfect football shape?) Back home, you pop a CD into the player. (How does the music get onto the disc?)

Life was very different a few centuries ago. If you were an average kid in the 1600s, you'd know a lot about your clothes and food and toys because you'd see them being made every day. You'd live in a rural community where the villagers made everything by hand. Your family would grow all its own food, and your mother would spin wool into yarn for clothes. Your toys would be bits of wood and string.

Ever since prehistoric hunter-gatherers roamed the Earth, people have used their hands and imaginations to make things they needed from the plants, animals, rocks and other natural materials around them. Then, in the 1700s, everything changed.

The Industrial Revolution transformed the making of things from an everyday community activity to a business run by machines in factories. The first product made this way was cloth, but soon many products were being turned out in factories. Manufacturing boomed as new machines and faster methods seemed to spring up overnight. The invention of steam engines was a great leap forward, since they could power ever bigger and more complicated machines.

Next came mass production. The American inventor Eli Whitney came up with the idea of having machines make identical parts of products and hiring unskilled workers to assemble them. Now, a musket, say, could be produced in a

fraction of the time it took an artisan to craft the parts and put them together by hand.

In the 1900s, Henry Ford developed the assembly line for building cars and trucks. Vehicles moved slowly along a line, and each worker attached one or more parts. From that time on, the people who built the thousands of products that rolled out of factories had little idea of how each piece was made or how everything fitted together.

Today, computers have dramatically changed manufacturing methods once again. In some factories, computer-operated machines and robots assemble entire products from start to finish, pack them into containers, and ship them off to stores.

Modern manufacturing has helped create a world that would seem miraculous to those villagers of a few centuries ago. They'd be stunned by the countless wonders we take for granted—from corn flakes and trainers to computer games and DVDs. Yet no matter how varied and complex these products are, they all still start out as pieces of the natural world.

Manufacturing begins with mining and harvesting raw materials such as oil, minerals and wood from the sea, land and forests. Making products out of these materials is generally done in two stages. In primary manufacturing, the raw materials are transformed into uniform pieces of timber, steel, plastic, glass or clay. In secondary manufacturing, these pieces may be melted, cut, crunched and often have their very molecules changed through the application of heat, pressure and chemicals. Bits and pieces are attached to other bits and pieces to make the final products.

In this book, we show you how sixty-nine familiar items are made today. You won't see here highly technical things like computer games and mobile phones, whose manufacture is too complex to explain on two pages. But you will find many old friends. You'll begin to unravel some of the mysteries around you – such as how plants and rocks become cans of cola, how trees are transformed into guitars, and why jeans are blue.

Fun and Games

11

Footballs

Football is the world's most popular game, largely because all you need to play is a ball. But the ball and the game have changed a lot over the years. In the Middle Ages, village teams used a pigskin ball stuffed with feathers. The teams had any number of players and the game could become violent.

The first modern footballs were made of eight leather panels sewn together. But after a while, the balls would stretch out of shape. Sixteen panels worked better, and today thirty-two panels are used.

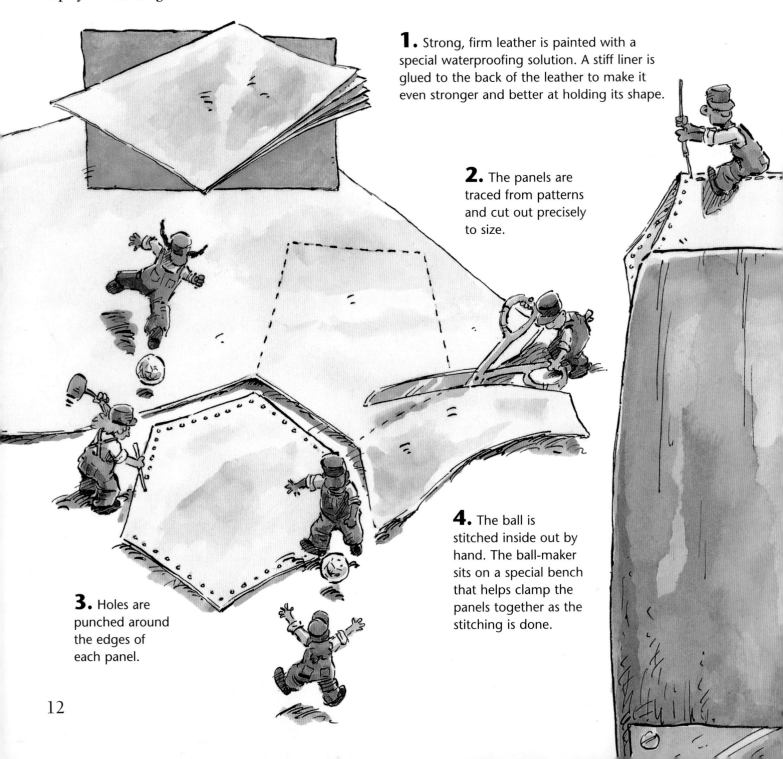

1. Strong, firm leather is painted with a special waterproofing solution. A stiff liner is glued to the back of the leather to make it even stronger and better at holding its shape.

2. The panels are traced from patterns and cut out precisely to size.

3. Holes are punched around the edges of each panel.

4. The ball is stitched inside out by hand. The ball-maker sits on a special bench that helps clamp the panels together as the stitching is done.

6. The ball-maker flattens out the seams with a hammer, making the ball as smooth and round as possible.

5. The thread is made of five strands twisted together and waxed to make it slide more easily through the holes. There is a needle at each end.

7. When the last seam is partly closed, the ball is turned right side out and a rubber bladder is stuffed inside. The valve on the bladder is left poking through a hole punched out in one of the panels.

8. After the last seam has been stitched up, the ball is inspected for quality and then inflated.

People have been kicking balls around for centuries, but football really became organized in the early 1800s in England. English schools had their own version of the rules, until they were standardized in 1863.

13

CDs

*D*o you play music when doing your homework? If so, you probably listen to compact discs (CDs). CDs give you better sound than any other technology – except for actual bands playing actual instruments in your house. And CDs are much more convenient than live bands!

1. A microphone captures the music. Audio equipment changes it into millions of tiny bits of digital sound and transfers it to a computer.

2. At the CD factory, the digital music is played, sending a signal to a laser. The laser is aimed at a spinning glass master disc that has been coated with a chemical 'resist'. As the laser turns on and off, the resist dissolves or stays, copying the exact pattern of the original sound.

3. The master is placed in a chemical bath that leaves the resist but etches pits in the exposed glass.

4. The master goes next into a silver bath, and electric current is applied, forming a thin layer of metal over the glass face (called electroforming). This metal copy is called the father.

9. The entire disc is then covered with a clear plastic protective coating. The CD is inspected again, labelled, packaged and shipped.

8. Each disc is covered with a very thin coating of aluminium.

7. The stampers are placed in moulds. Melted plastic is injected into the moulds to produce clear plastic discs, containing digital tracks on one side only (*see* Plastic Resins, page 152).

6. The stampers are trimmed to the right size. They have their centre holes punched out and are inspected for flaws.

5. Using electroforming, one or more metal 'mothers' are made from the father. Each mother produces a 'son' (also called a stamper).

Father

Father

Mother

Father

Mother

Son

Master

Do you see a family resemblance?

Like father, like son.

15

Chewing Gum

It is 1869, and Thomas Adams and his son, Tom Junior, are in the family workshop, scratching their heads over a big barrel of dried sap from a Mexican jungle tree. They have ordered this 'chicle' hoping to make a new kind of rubber for tyres. But it just isn't working out. Absentmindedly, Thomas tears off a piece and starts chewing it. 'Hey – not bad!' Soon they have built a factory to produce sticks of 'Adams' New York Gum No. 1'.

Today's chewing gum is made roughly as Thomas and Tom Junior did it.

1. Natural latex (from trees) or artificial latex comes to the gum factory in large blocks, which are ground into small chunks and placed in a warm dry room for a few days.

2. When dry, the gum (chicle) is cooked in a kettle until it melts. It is processed to remove any insects, bark or other impurities, and then cooked in another kettle, where the gum is stirred with powdered sugar, corn syrup, colour, flavourings and softeners.

3. The cooked mixture is cooled and then kneaded for several hours to the right texture.

Double, double,
Toil and trouble,
Fire burn and
Cauldron bubble!

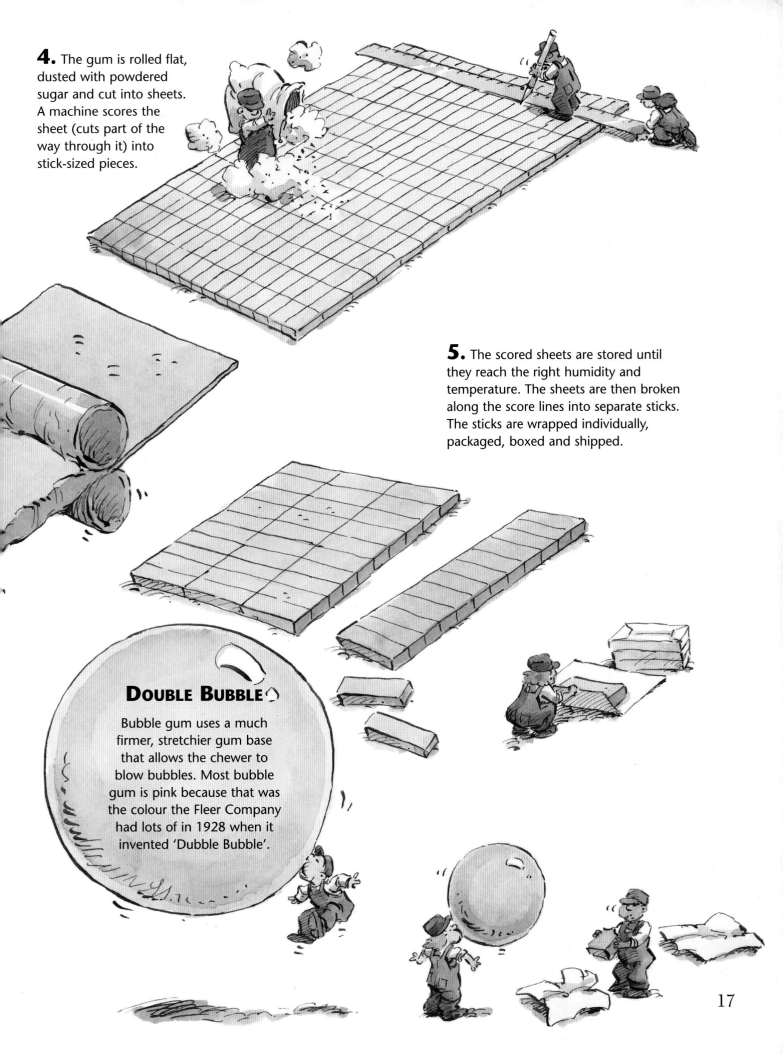

4. The gum is rolled flat, dusted with powdered sugar and cut into sheets. A machine scores the sheet (cuts part of the way through it) into stick-sized pieces.

5. The scored sheets are stored until they reach the right humidity and temperature. The sheets are then broken along the score lines into separate sticks. The sticks are wrapped individually, packaged, boxed and shipped.

DOUBLE BUBBLE

Bubble gum uses a much firmer, stretchier gum base that allows the chewer to blow bubbles. Most bubble gum is pink because that was the colour the Fleer Company had lots of in 1928 when it invented 'Dubble Bubble'.

Dolls

Today, dolls are kids' stuff. But in ancient Egypt, they represented religious gods and goddesses and were buried with the dead to be servants in the afterlife. These were not dolls to be played with. Even in Japan today, dolls are used to teach children about their history and culture.

Throughout history, dolls have been made from grass, leather, clay and wood. Doll makers have also used wax, papier mâché, porcelain and 'composition', a blend of glue and sawdust. When plastic came into use in the 1940s, it took over as the main doll-making material.

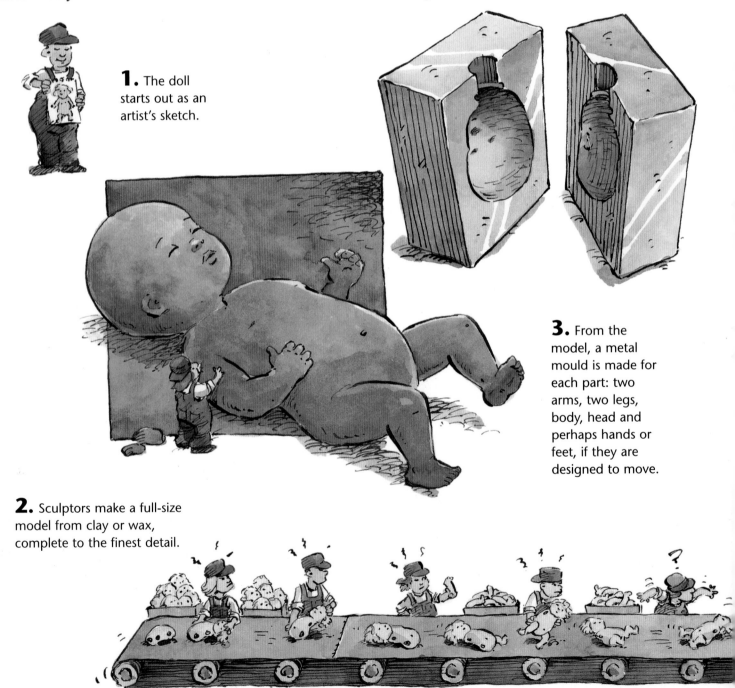

1. The doll starts out as an artist's sketch.

2. Sculptors make a full-size model from clay or wax, complete to the finest detail.

3. From the model, a metal mould is made for each part: two arms, two legs, body, head and perhaps hands or feet, if they are designed to move.

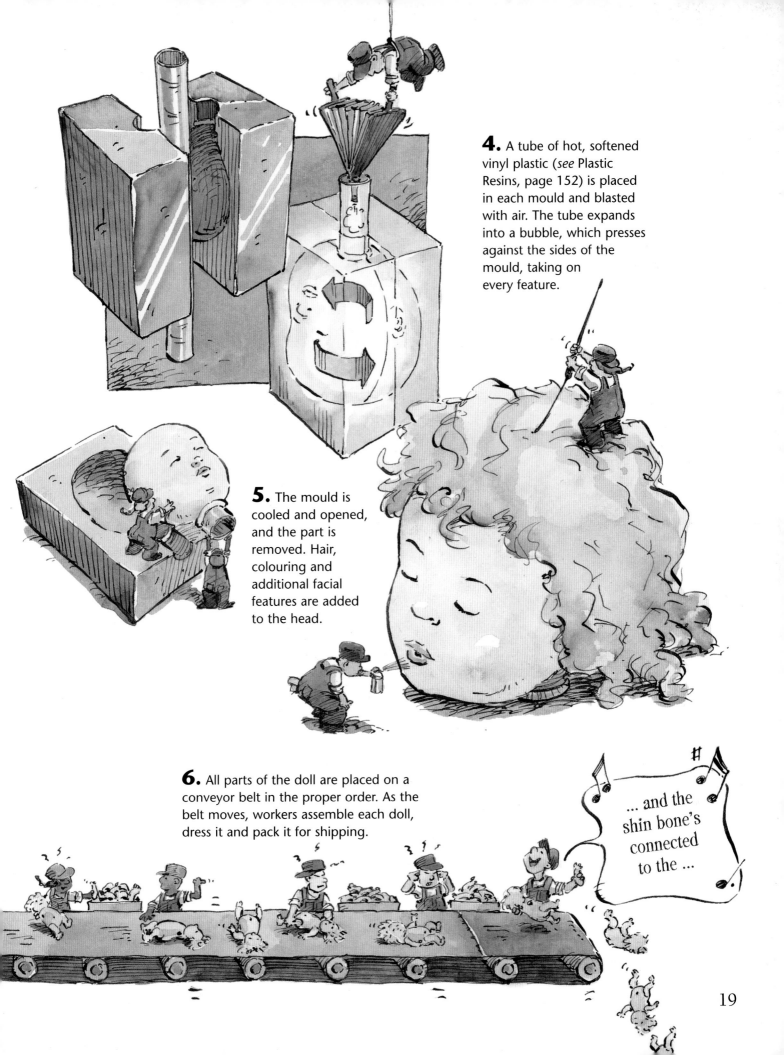

4. A tube of hot, softened vinyl plastic (*see* Plastic Resins, page 152) is placed in each mould and blasted with air. The tube expands into a bubble, which presses against the sides of the mould, taking on every feature.

5. The mould is cooled and opened, and the part is removed. Hair, colouring and additional facial features are added to the head.

6. All parts of the doll are placed on a conveyor belt in the proper order. As the belt moves, workers assemble each doll, dress it and pack it for shipping.

... and the shin bone's connected to the ...

19

American Footballs

The earliest form of football in North America was played in the colony of Virginia in 1609. A blown-up pig's bladder served as the ball. In American football today the ball has little to do with a pig. To make one, what you really need is a cow ...

1. Four leather panels are cut out to make each ball. The inside is lined with cotton. One panel is stamped with the company name.

2. Two of the panels are marked to show where the laces will go, and pieces of rubber-covered fabric are attached to these areas.

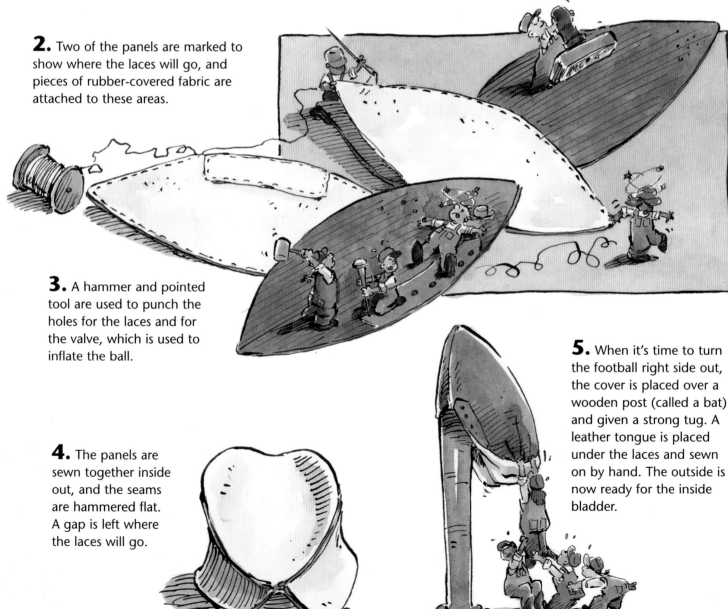

3. A hammer and pointed tool are used to punch the holes for the laces and for the valve, which is used to inflate the ball.

5. When it's time to turn the football right side out, the cover is placed over a wooden post (called a bat) and given a strong tug. A leather tongue is placed under the laces and sewn on by hand. The outside is now ready for the inside bladder.

4. The panels are sewn together inside out, and the seams are hammered flat. A gap is left where the laces will go.

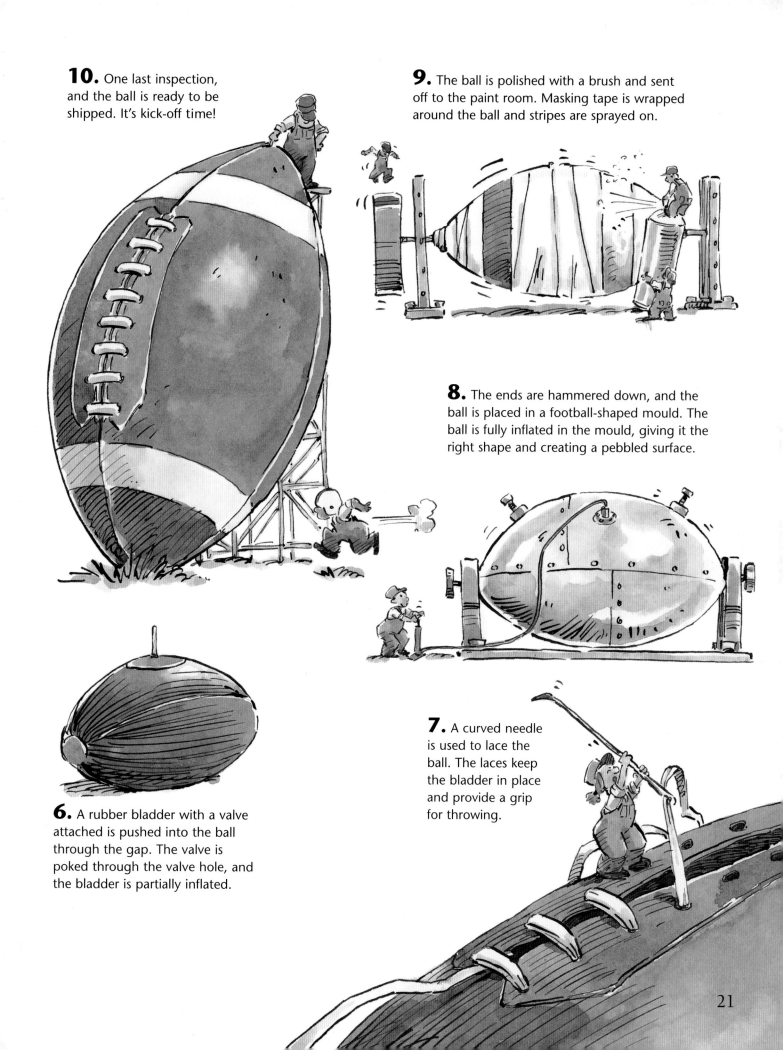

10. One last inspection, and the ball is ready to be shipped. It's kick-off time!

9. The ball is polished with a brush and sent off to the paint room. Masking tape is wrapped around the ball and stripes are sprayed on.

8. The ends are hammered down, and the ball is placed in a football-shaped mould. The ball is fully inflated in the mould, giving it the right shape and creating a pebbled surface.

7. A curved needle is used to lace the ball. The laces keep the bladder in place and provide a grip for throwing.

6. A rubber bladder with a valve attached is pushed into the ball through the gap. The valve is poked through the valve hole, and the bladder is partially inflated.

21

Guitars

Can you imagine carrying a piano around in a case? That's one reason the guitar has become so popular – it's portable!

In ancient times, Middle Eastern people carved pictures of a stringed instrument that had a neck, a sound hole and curved sides. By the 1200s, musicians in Spain were playing the four-stringed *guitarra latina*. By 1800, guitar makers had added the fifth and the sixth string, the thick bass E.

Here's how classical acoustic guitars are made.

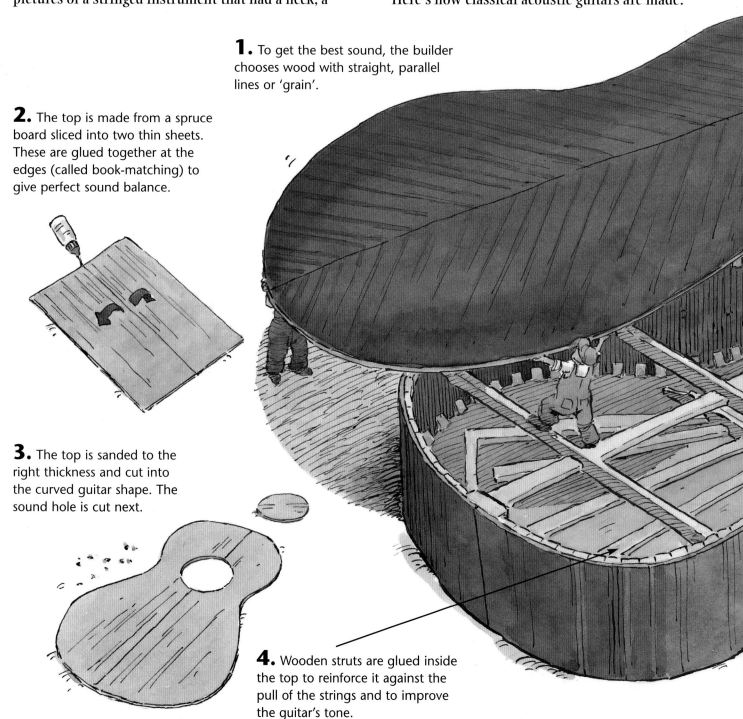

1. To get the best sound, the builder chooses wood with straight, parallel lines or 'grain'.

2. The top is made from a spruce board sliced into two thin sheets. These are glued together at the edges (called book-matching) to give perfect sound balance.

3. The top is sanded to the right thickness and cut into the curved guitar shape. The sound hole is cut next.

4. Wooden struts are glued inside the top to reinforce it against the pull of the strings and to improve the guitar's tone.

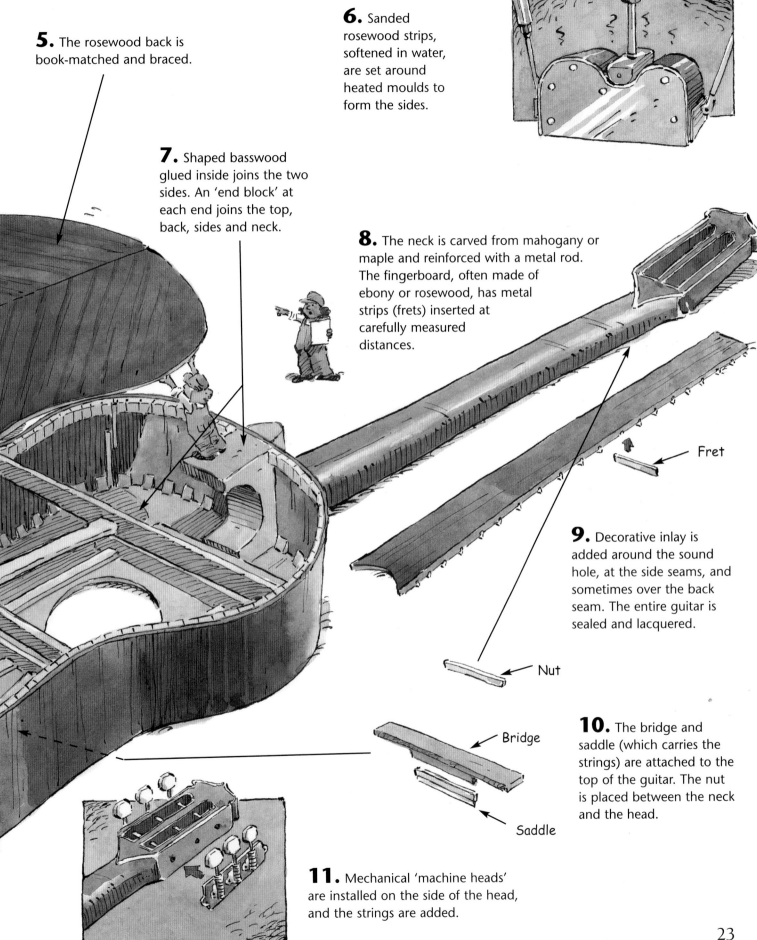

5. The rosewood back is book-matched and braced.

6. Sanded rosewood strips, softened in water, are set around heated moulds to form the sides.

7. Shaped basswood glued inside joins the two sides. An 'end block' at each end joins the top, back, sides and neck.

8. The neck is carved from mahogany or maple and reinforced with a metal rod. The fingerboard, often made of ebony or rosewood, has metal strips (frets) inserted at carefully measured distances.

9. Decorative inlay is added around the sound hole, at the side seams, and sometimes over the back seam. The entire guitar is sealed and lacquered.

Fret

Nut

Bridge

Saddle

10. The bridge and saddle (which carries the strings) are attached to the top of the guitar. The nut is placed between the neck and the head.

11. Mechanical 'machine heads' are installed on the side of the head, and the strings are added.

Marbles

Agates, shooters and cat's-eyes – kids have played games with small round balls forever, it seems. The child king Tutankhamen of Egypt took marbles to his tomb. Greek and Roman children played with marbles made of clay. And marbles have been discovered in ancient Native American burial sites.

In Germany in the early 1600s, marbles were made of actual marble. Glass was probably first used in Venice, where Italian craftspeople shaped the marbles by hand. The first machine-made marbles in North America were produced in a barn in Ohio in the early 1900s.

1. At a high temperature, sand, soda lime and silica are melted and mixed together. Crushed glass 'cullet' is also melted and mixed in (*see* Glass, page 142).

ROLLING OUT THE MARBLES

A marble factory in Mexico makes about 12 million marbles a day.

2. The mixture is poured into a flow tank, and melted coloured glass is pumped in. Mixing all these materials together gives the marbles their special colours and patterns.

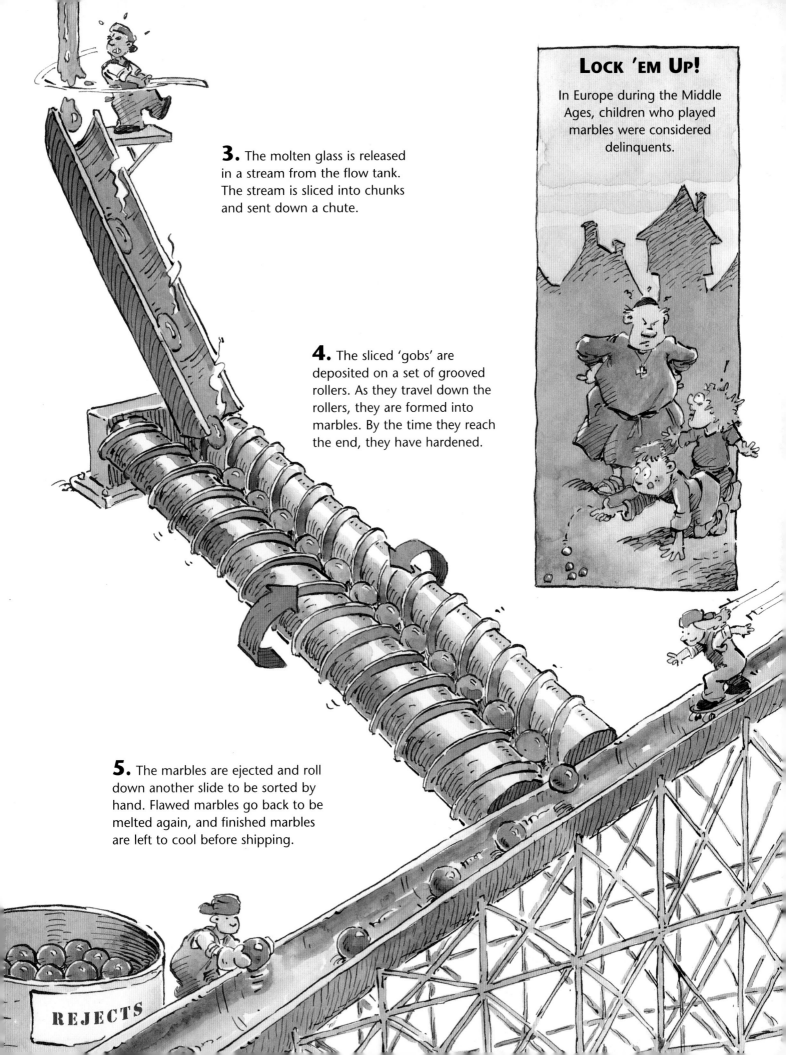

3. The molten glass is released in a stream from the flow tank. The stream is sliced into chunks and sent down a chute.

4. The sliced 'gobs' are deposited on a set of grooved rollers. As they travel down the rollers, they are formed into marbles. By the time they reach the end, they have hardened.

5. The marbles are ejected and roll down another slide to be sorted by hand. Flawed marbles go back to be melted again, and finished marbles are left to cool before shipping.

LOCK 'EM UP!

In Europe during the Middle Ages, children who played marbles were considered delinquents.

REJECTS

Neon Signs

Do you like to 'see the bright lights'? Part of the fun of being in town at night is enjoying the lights that brighten up theatres, shops and restaurants. And the most dramatic of those lights are neon signs. Combining science and art, neon signs get their messages across with letters and shapes of pure coloured light that comes from a gas. Neon was the first gas used in these wonderful signs, though now it is one of many.

Neon gas is naturally present in the air in tiny amounts. British scientists William Ramsey and M. W. Travers discovered it accidentally in 1898 when they were working on a method to separate oxygen from liquid air and got neon as well. Around 1902, a Frenchman named Georges Claude found a cheaper way to extract the new gas and went on to create the first glowing neon lamp.

1. A sign-maker draws the design and transfers it to a sheet of asbestos. This will be the guide for bending the glass tubes.

2. The glass tubing (*see* Glass, page 142) is cleaned. If a gas other than neon or argon is to be used (such as krypton or xenon), the tube is then placed in a machine that blows liquid phosphor into it and lets it drain dry. The phosphor coating will make the light shine brighter.

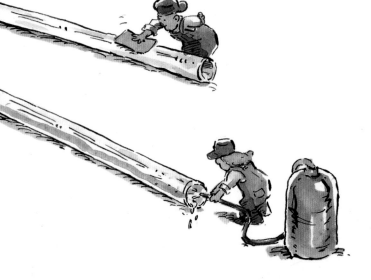

3. The sign-maker heats the tube to soften it and make it easy to bend in the right places. At the same time, she blows into the tube to keep it from collapsing. She works with bare hands in order to feel when the temperature of the glass is right for bending.

4. A metal electrode is heated and fused to each end of the glass tube. Special paint is applied to mask the parts of the sign that are not meant to shine.

5. The air is pumped out through a small hole at the end of the electrode. An electrical current flows through the tube, heating it and the electrodes to a very high temperature, and forcing out impurities.

6. The tube is cooled, and the desired gas (neon for red or orange, argon for blue) is pumped in at low pressure. The hole is sealed.

Electrode

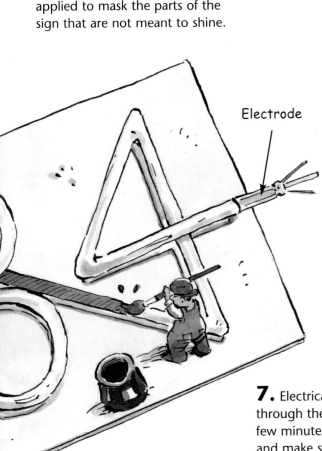

7. Electrical current is passed through the gas-filled tube for a few minutes to stabilize the gas and make sure it operates properly. This step is called burning-in.

8. The sign is attached to the frame, and the electrical wiring is hooked up to a transformer to operate the light.

FLASHY COLOURS

The brightness and colour of the light are the result of gas electrons within the atom getting bumped out of their orbit by the electrical current. When they bounce back, they give off a flash of energy in the form of coloured light. Various combinations of gases and coatings inside the tube can produce more than fifty different colours.

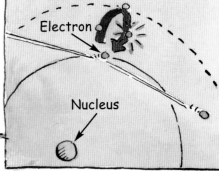

Electron

Nucleus

27

Plastic Dinosaurs

Do plastic dinosaurs create a miniature world for you, where *T. Rex* and the pterodactyls rule the planet – or at least your living room?

We all know the real giant lizards were cold-blooded and started out as eggs, but what about the plastic versions?

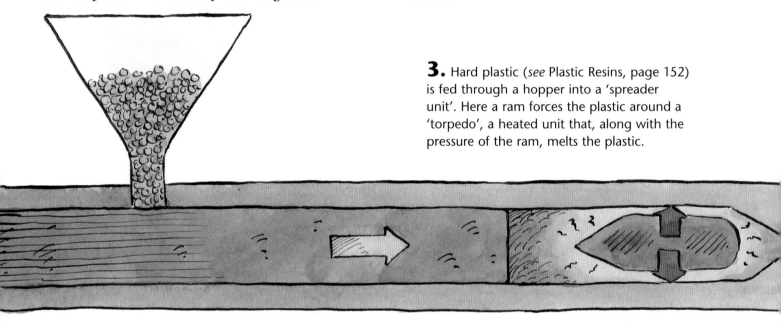

3. Hard plastic (*see* Plastic Resins, page 152) is fed through a hopper into a 'spreader unit'. Here a ram forces the plastic around a 'torpedo', a heated unit that, along with the pressure of the ram, melts the plastic.

1. An artist designs the dinosaur toy, and then a sculptor makes a model from clay or wax, including lots of details.

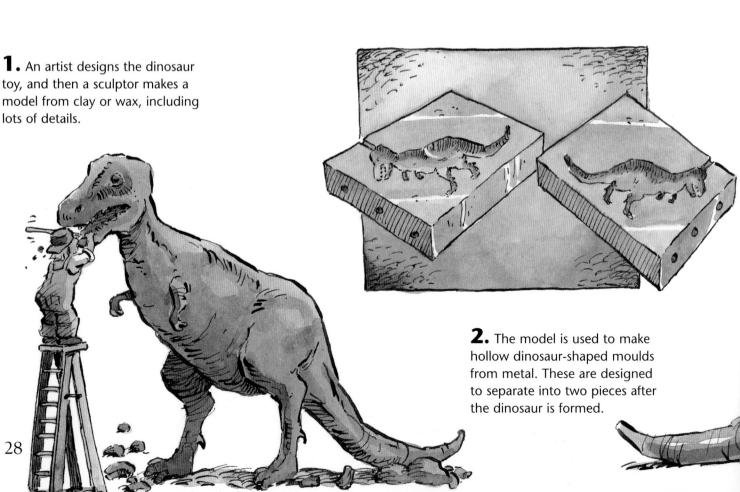

2. The model is used to make hollow dinosaur-shaped moulds from metal. These are designed to separate into two pieces after the dinosaur is formed.

4. The melted plastic is forced through a nozzle and into a channel that carries the plastic into the mould.

5. After cold air or water is applied to cool it, the mould is opened and the dinosaur pops out. A worker inspects the toy for flaws and may finish it by snipping off extra plastic or painting on colours or lines.

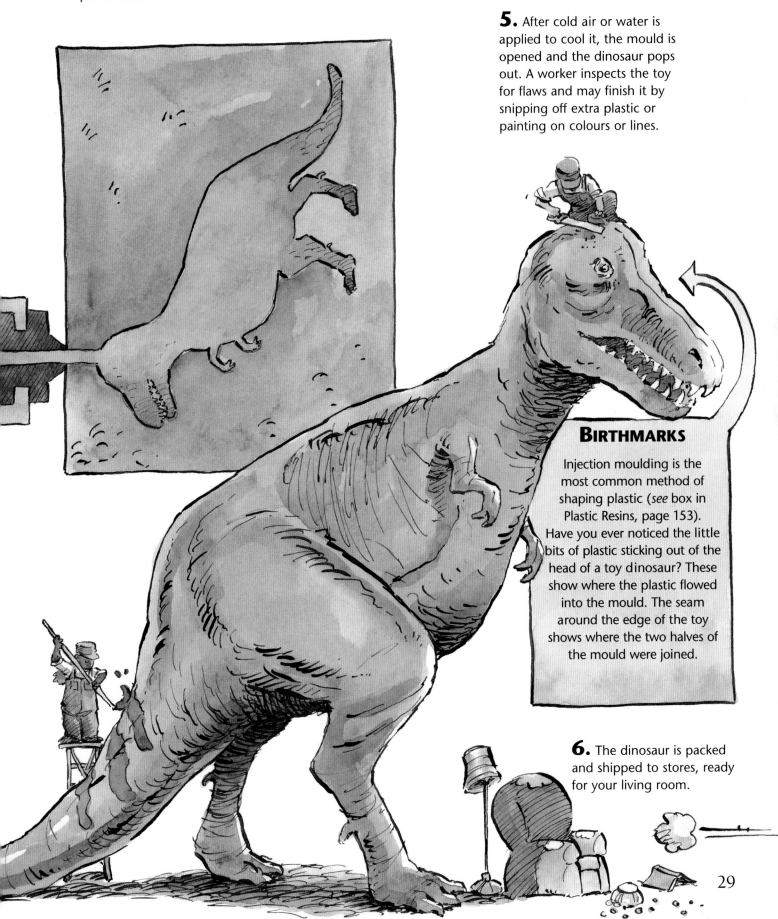

BIRTHMARKS

Injection moulding is the most common method of shaping plastic (*see* box in Plastic Resins, page 153). Have you ever noticed the little bits of plastic sticking out of the head of a toy dinosaur? These show where the plastic flowed into the mould. The seam around the edge of the toy shows where the two halves of the mould were joined.

6. The dinosaur is packed and shipped to stores, ready for your living room.

29

Ship in a Bottle

Have you ever tried to squeeze toothpaste back into the tube? Getting a model sailing ship inside a bottle must be just about as hard. How do they do it?

People first asked that question in the 1800s, when sailors began building miniature ships in glass bottles as an enjoyable way to pass the time on long ocean voyages.

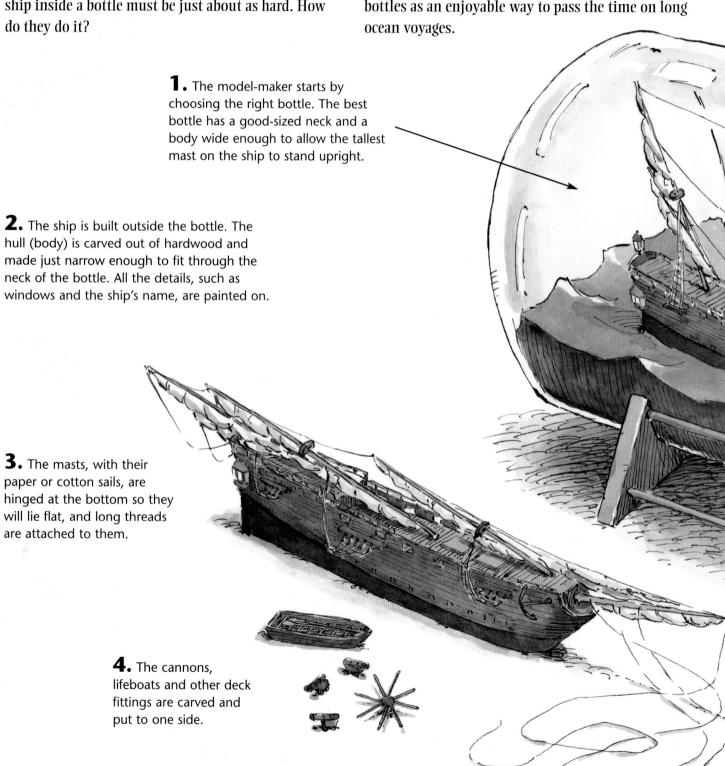

1. The model-maker starts by choosing the right bottle. The best bottle has a good-sized neck and a body wide enough to allow the tallest mast on the ship to stand upright.

2. The ship is built outside the bottle. The hull (body) is carved out of hardwood and made just narrow enough to fit through the neck of the bottle. All the details, such as windows and the ship's name, are painted on.

3. The masts, with their paper or cotton sails, are hinged at the bottom so they will lie flat, and long threads are attached to them.

4. The cannons, lifeboats and other deck fittings are carved and put to one side.

5. The model-maker uses a long rod to press blue modelling clay into the bottle to look like the sea.

6. He slides the ship into the bottle stern first so a key thread connected to the bowsprit is in the correct position. The threads are long enough to hang out of the neck of the bottle.

Bowsprit

7. The builder gently pulls on the threads to draw the masts upright. Sails are unrolled, and with a thin rod dabbed in quick-drying glue, he anchors the threads, sails and deck fittings in place.

Heave, me laddies!

8. Using a rod with a sharp blade on the end, he trims off any unwanted threads. He corks the bottle to keep out dust, and the model is ready to sail.

31

Baseballs

Have you ever knocked the cover off a soggy old baseball and found a bewildering ball of yarn inside that scrap of leather? If you have, you've only just begun to unravel the mystery of this thing we call a baseball.

The first baseballs were a rock or a walnut wound with string, cloth or even old socks, and covered with stitched-up shoe leather.

1. At the core of today's baseball is the 'pill' – a cork sphere cushioned with separate red and black layers of rubber (*see* Rubber, page 156).

2. Wound around the pill are three layers of coloured woollen yarn (blue-grey, white, blue-grey) and a layer of white polycotton yarn. Nearly 400 m (over 1300 ft.) of yarn is packed inside a single baseball.

3. The centre is now dipped in a bath of rubber-based glue, and is ready to receive its cover.

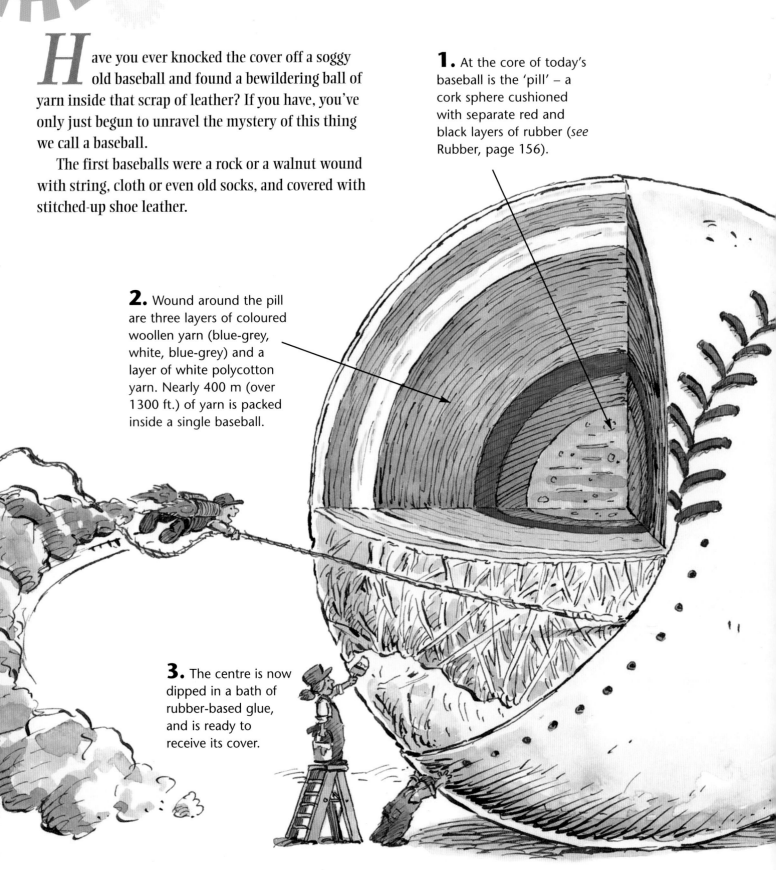

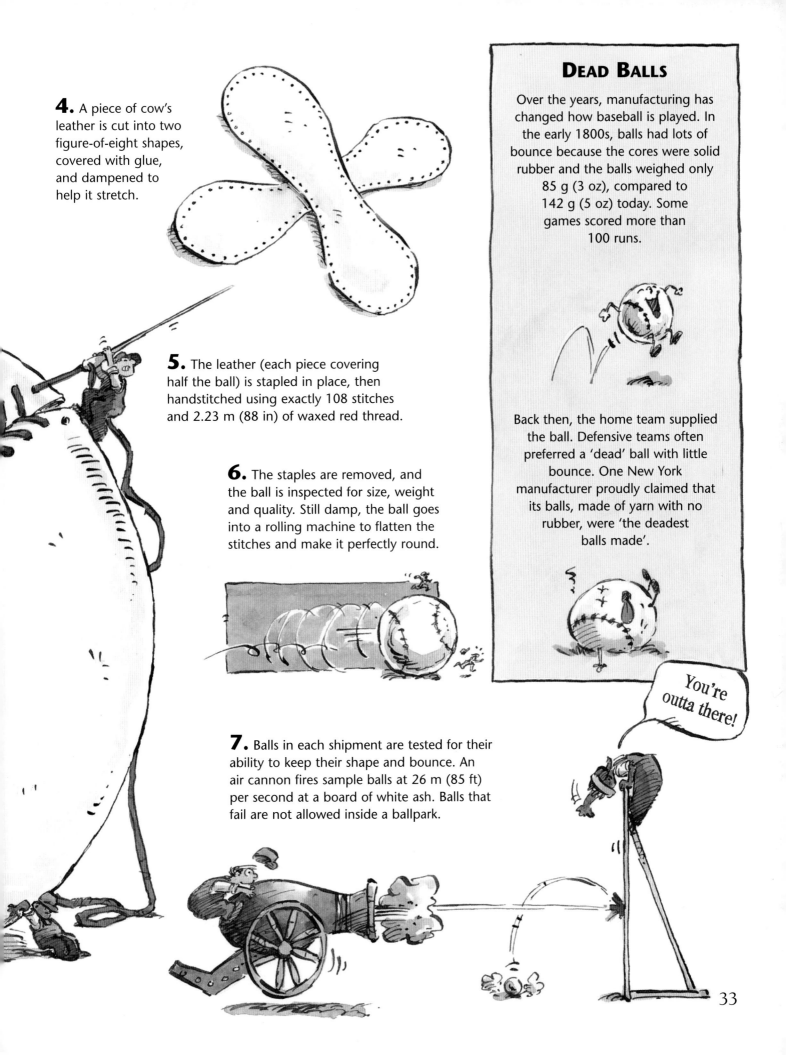

4. A piece of cow's leather is cut into two figure-of-eight shapes, covered with glue, and dampened to help it stretch.

5. The leather (each piece covering half the ball) is stapled in place, then handstitched using exactly 108 stitches and 2.23 m (88 in) of waxed red thread.

6. The staples are removed, and the ball is inspected for size, weight and quality. Still damp, the ball goes into a rolling machine to flatten the stitches and make it perfectly round.

7. Balls in each shipment are tested for their ability to keep their shape and bounce. An air cannon fires sample balls at 26 m (85 ft) per second at a board of white ash. Balls that fail are not allowed inside a ballpark.

DEAD BALLS

Over the years, manufacturing has changed how baseball is played. In the early 1800s, balls had lots of bounce because the cores were solid rubber and the balls weighed only 85 g (3 oz), compared to 142 g (5 oz) today. Some games scored more than 100 runs.

Back then, the home team supplied the ball. Defensive teams often preferred a 'dead' ball with little bounce. One New York manufacturer proudly claimed that its balls, made of yarn with no rubber, were 'the deadest balls made'.

You're outta there!

33

Surfboards

When you learn how to do it, surfing can give you a roller coaster of a ride – but watch out for the curl of the wave!

People in Polynesia and Hawaii have been surfing for hundreds of years, at first using very heavy boards carved out of solid tree trunks. Surfboards are now made of lightweight material that floats well but is strong enough to carry the weight of the surfer and withstand the power of the waves.

High-end custom surfboards start out as pieces of polyurethane foam called blanks.

1. To make the blank, liquid foam is poured into a cement mould. The mould is heated, and blowing agents (chemicals) in the foam make it expand to fill the mould.

4. A shaper uses saws, planes and sandpaper to trim and smooth the board to its final shape.

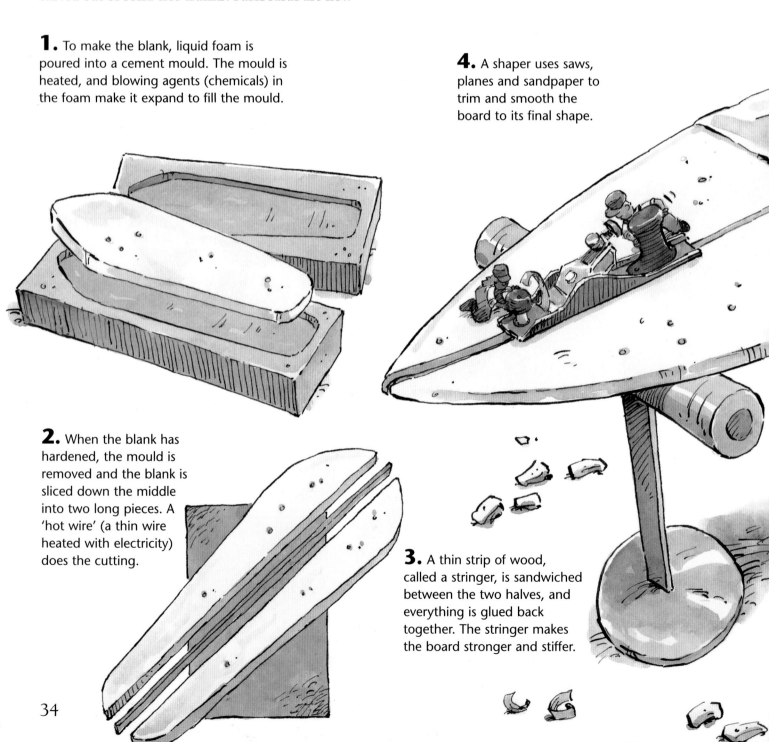

2. When the blank has hardened, the mould is removed and the blank is sliced down the middle into two long pieces. A 'hot wire' (a thin wire heated with electricity) does the cutting.

3. A thin strip of wood, called a stringer, is sandwiched between the two halves, and everything is glued back together. The stringer makes the board stronger and stiffer.

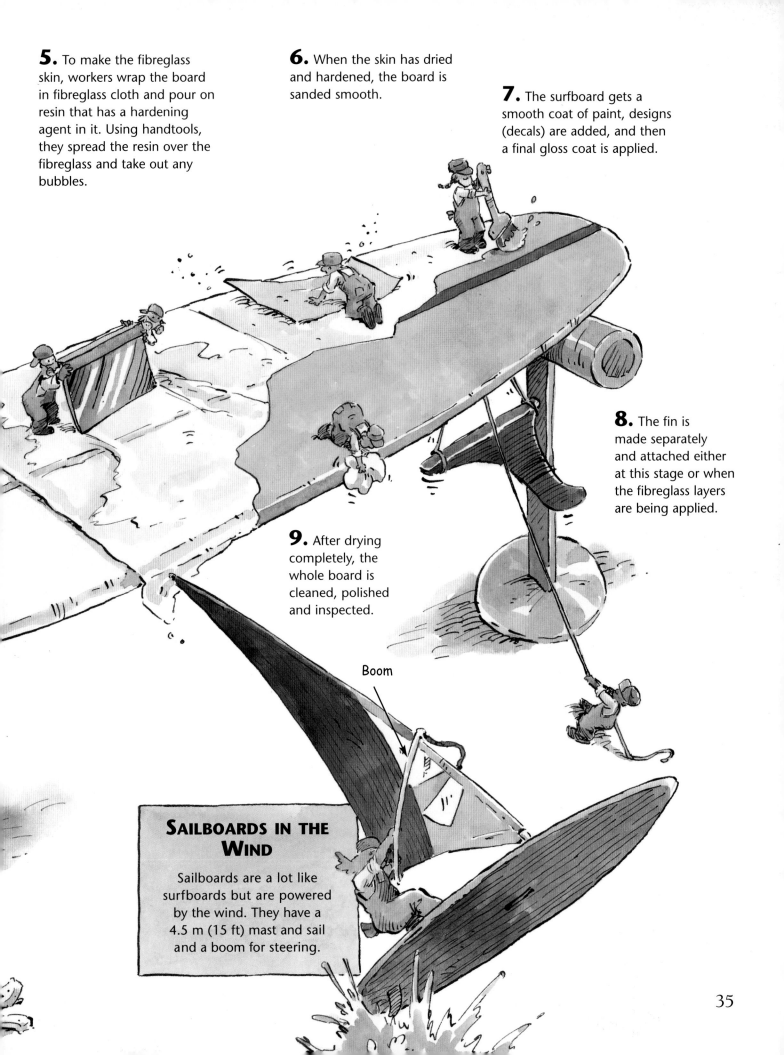

5. To make the fibreglass skin, workers wrap the board in fibreglass cloth and pour on resin that has a hardening agent in it. Using handtools, they spread the resin over the fibreglass and take out any bubbles.

6. When the skin has dried and hardened, the board is sanded smooth.

7. The surfboard gets a smooth coat of paint, designs (decals) are added, and then a final gloss coat is applied.

8. The fin is made separately and attached either at this stage or when the fibreglass layers are being applied.

9. After drying completely, the whole board is cleaned, polished and inspected.

Boom

SAILBOARDS IN THE WIND

Sailboards are a lot like surfboards but are powered by the wind. They have a 4.5 m (15 ft) mast and sail and a boom for steering.

Teddy Bears

The American president Theodore ('Teddy') Roosevelt really started something when he went bear hunting in 1902. A newspaper cartoon making fun of the hunt gave a New York shopkeeper named Morris Michtom an idea for a product. He asked his wife to make some stuffed toy bears from brown plush fabric. Customers loved 'Teddy's Bears', so Mr Michtom formed the Ideal Novelty and Toy Corporation to produce them.

Strangely enough, that same year the Steiff company in Germany also created a stuffed bear, which it introduced at the Leipzig Toy Fair. By 1906, both companies were calling their toys teddy bears and selling them by the hundreds of thousands.

1. A cutting machine cuts out the parts for the head, ears, body, legs and arms from imitation fur fabric.

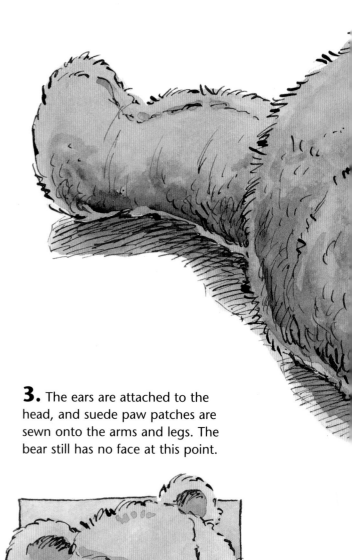

2. Industrial sewing machines join the seams on the reverse side of the fur. An opening is left in each part, which is then turned right side out. All parts but the body are stuffed and stitched up.

3. The ears are attached to the head, and suede paw patches are sewn onto the arms and legs. The bear still has no face at this point.

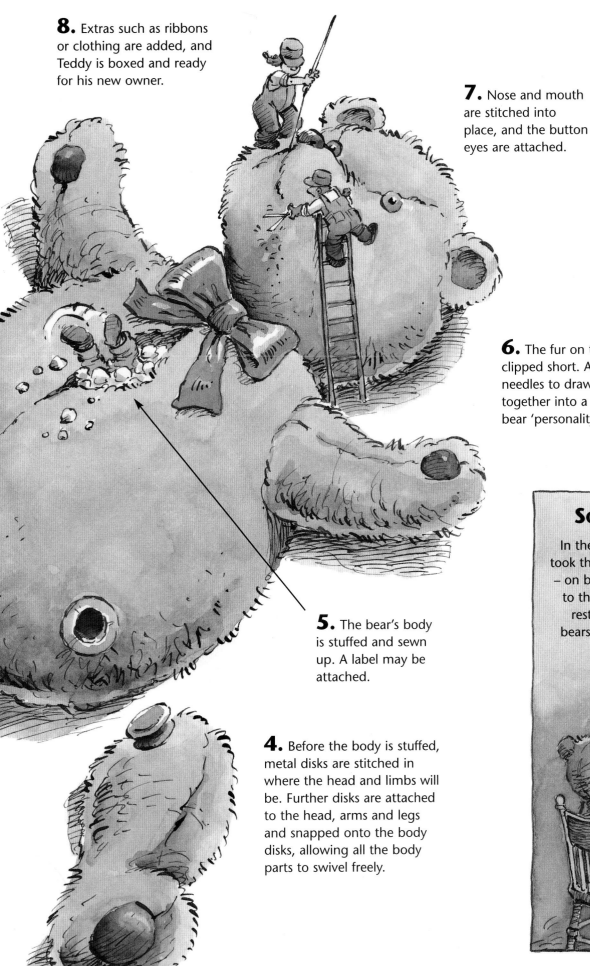

8. Extras such as ribbons or clothing are added, and Teddy is boxed and ready for his new owner.

7. Nose and mouth are stitched into place, and the button eyes are attached.

6. The fur on the bear's face is clipped short. A sewer uses long needles to draw the material together into a snout, giving the bear 'personality'.

5. The bear's body is stuffed and sewn up. A label may be attached.

4. Before the body is stuffed, metal disks are stitched in where the head and limbs will be. Further disks are attached to the head, arms and legs and snapped onto the body disks, allowing all the body parts to swivel freely.

SOCIAL TEDDY

In the early 1900s, people took their teddies everywhere – on bicycle trips, to parties, to the beach and even to restaurants, where the bears got their own chairs at the table.

Whistles

The first modern whistle came on the scene in 1878 as a better way for British football referees to signal. The old way, waving a piece of cloth, was not very helpful for fans who could not see the official.

Recognizing a good thing when they heard it, the London police adopted the whistle a few years later to replace what they had been using to alert lawbreakers – a hand rattle. Today, whistles are used by campers, sailors, lifeguards and anyone else who wants to attract people's attention.

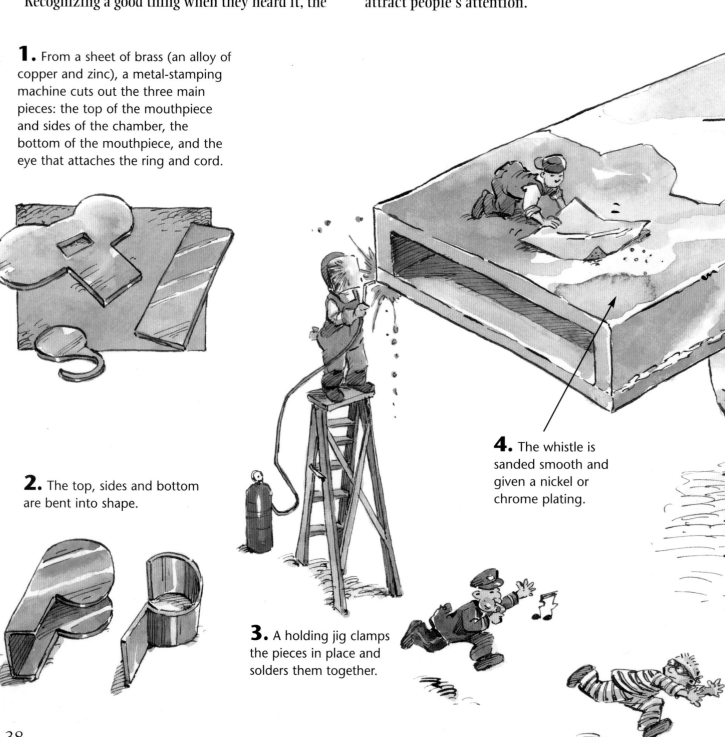

1. From a sheet of brass (an alloy of copper and zinc), a metal-stamping machine cuts out the three main pieces: the top of the mouthpiece and sides of the chamber, the bottom of the mouthpiece, and the eye that attaches the ring and cord.

2. The top, sides and bottom are bent into shape.

3. A holding jig clamps the pieces in place and solders them together.

4. The whistle is sanded smooth and given a nickel or chrome plating.

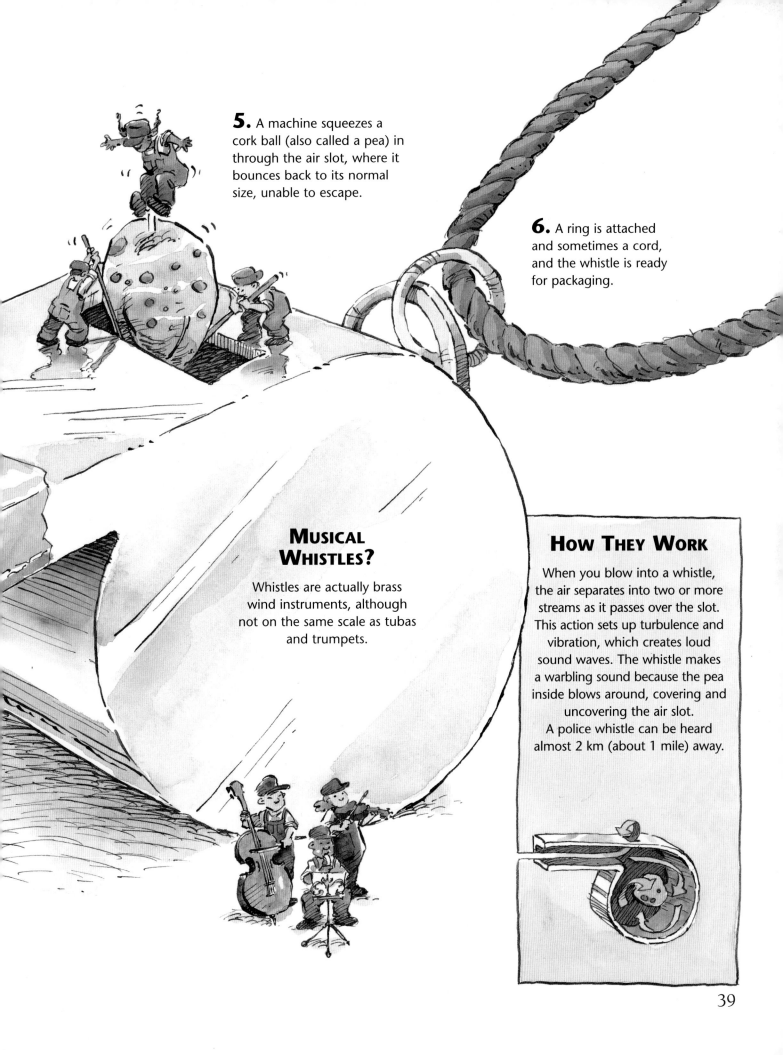

5. A machine squeezes a cork ball (also called a pea) in through the air slot, where it bounces back to its normal size, unable to escape.

6. A ring is attached and sometimes a cord, and the whistle is ready for packaging.

MUSICAL WHISTLES?

Whistles are actually brass wind instruments, although not on the same scale as tubas and trumpets.

HOW THEY WORK

When you blow into a whistle, the air separates into two or more streams as it passes over the slot. This action sets up turbulence and vibration, which creates loud sound waves. The whistle makes a warbling sound because the pea inside blows around, covering and uncovering the air slot.

A police whistle can be heard almost 2 km (about 1 mile) away.

Around the House

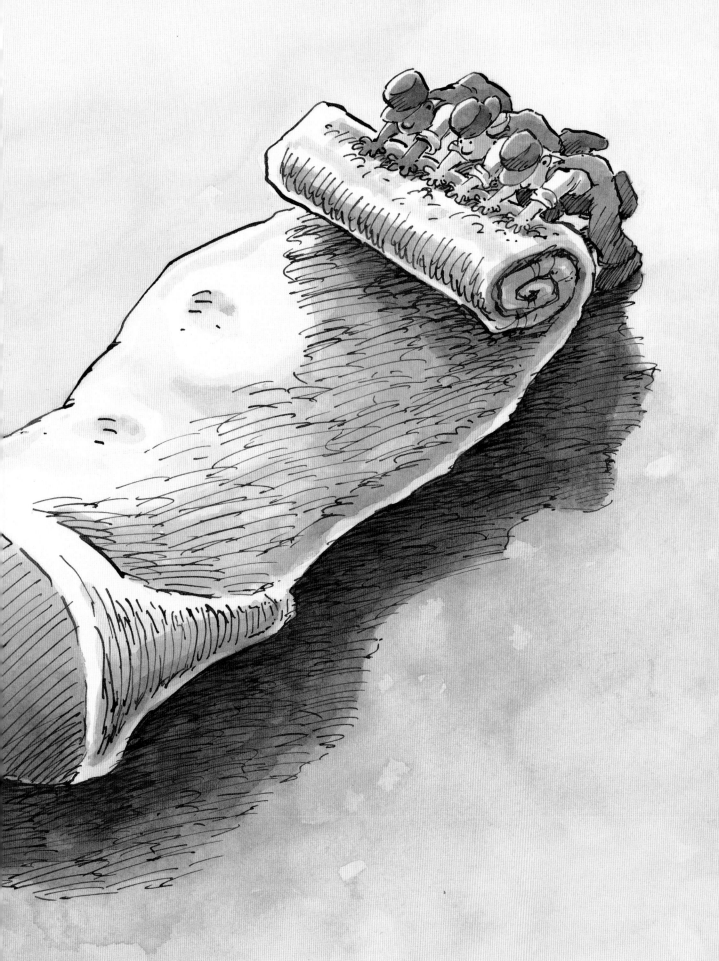

Aluminium Foil

Almost every house contains a roll of aluminium foil. It's a great food protector because it keeps out light, air and moisture, and is non-toxic. Foil is used in many crafts, and rolled into a ball, it makes one of the best possible cat toys!

About 5000 years ago, in what is now northern Iraq, people flattened out clay containing aluminium ore (*see* Aluminium, page 136) into thin sheets to make hard, durable pottery. The problem was you couldn't wrap the left-over roast goat in it. Thin, flexible aluminium foil didn't come along until 1903 in France and ten years later in the United States. One of its first uses was to make leg bands for passenger pigeons.

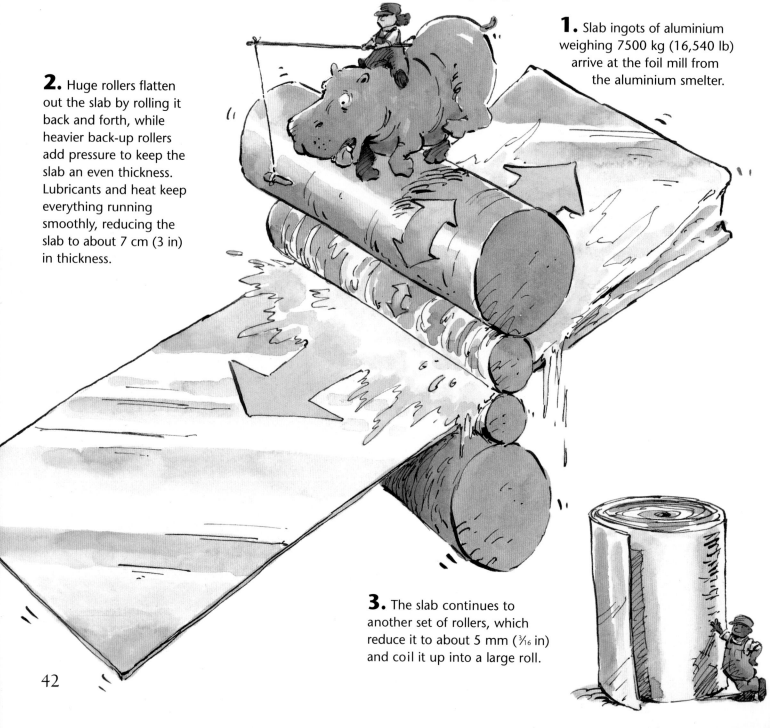

1. Slab ingots of aluminium weighing 7500 kg (16,540 lb) arrive at the foil mill from the aluminium smelter.

2. Huge rollers flatten out the slab by rolling it back and forth, while heavier back-up rollers add pressure to keep the slab an even thickness. Lubricants and heat keep everything running smoothly, reducing the slab to about 7 cm (3 in) in thickness.

3. The slab continues to another set of rollers, which reduce it to about 5 mm (³⁄₁₆ in) and coil it up into a large roll.

4. This foil stock now goes to the cold-roller mill. Another series of rollers reduce the foil to less than the thickness of a hair, at temperatures of about 100 °C (212 °F), to keep the foil flexible.

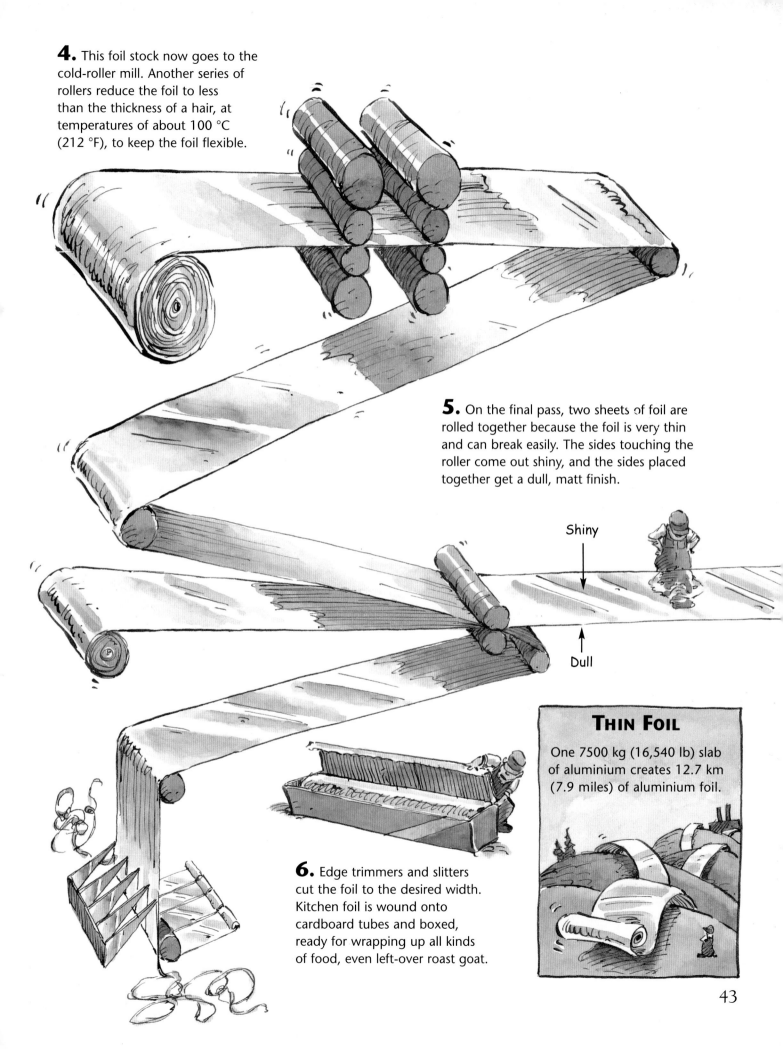

5. On the final pass, two sheets of foil are rolled together because the foil is very thin and can break easily. The sides touching the roller come out shiny, and the sides placed together get a dull, matt finish.

Shiny

Dull

THIN FOIL

One 7500 kg (16,540 lb) slab of aluminium creates 12.7 km (7.9 miles) of aluminium foil.

6. Edge trimmers and slitters cut the foil to the desired width. Kitchen foil is wound onto cardboard tubes and boxed, ready for wrapping up all kinds of food, even left-over roast goat.

Books

The earliest 'books' were scrolls made from papyrus (a reedy water plant) wrapped around a stick. In the Middle Ages, monks used to handwrite and illustrate books with flat paper sheets and wooden covers. Then in the mid-1400s, a German printer named Johannes Gutenberg invented movable metal type, making it possible to print books much faster and more easily. And new technologies are still changing the way books are made.

Books go through a long process of writing, editing and design before they are ready for printing.

1. Computer files of the book's words and graphics (pictures) go to a laser system that creates a photographic negative for each page. The negatives are transferred onto metal printing plates. A different plate is produced for each colour of ink needed, usually four (blue, red, yellow and black).

2. The plates are wrapped around cylinders in a printing press. The plate cylinder turns the plate against a roller that dampens the areas where ink is not wanted. Then it rotates against an inking roller that inks only the dry areas of the plate.

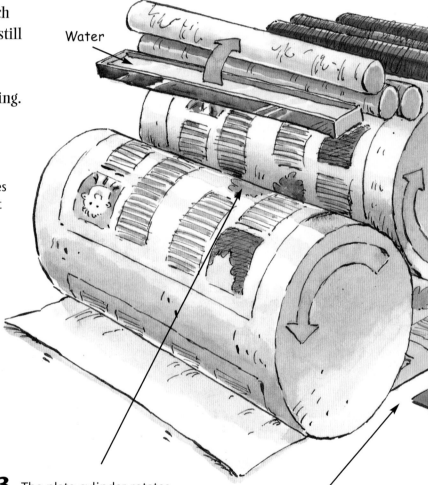

Water

3. The plate cylinder rotates against a rubber 'blanket' cylinder and deposits (offsets) ink onto it. The blanket cylinder transfers the ink to paper. This kind of printing, where ink is transferred from a plate to a blanket to paper, is called offset printing.

4. Paper is fed through the press in single sheets, as shown here, or in large rolls. One side is printed and allowed to dry. Then the sheet is fed through a second time to print the reverse side.

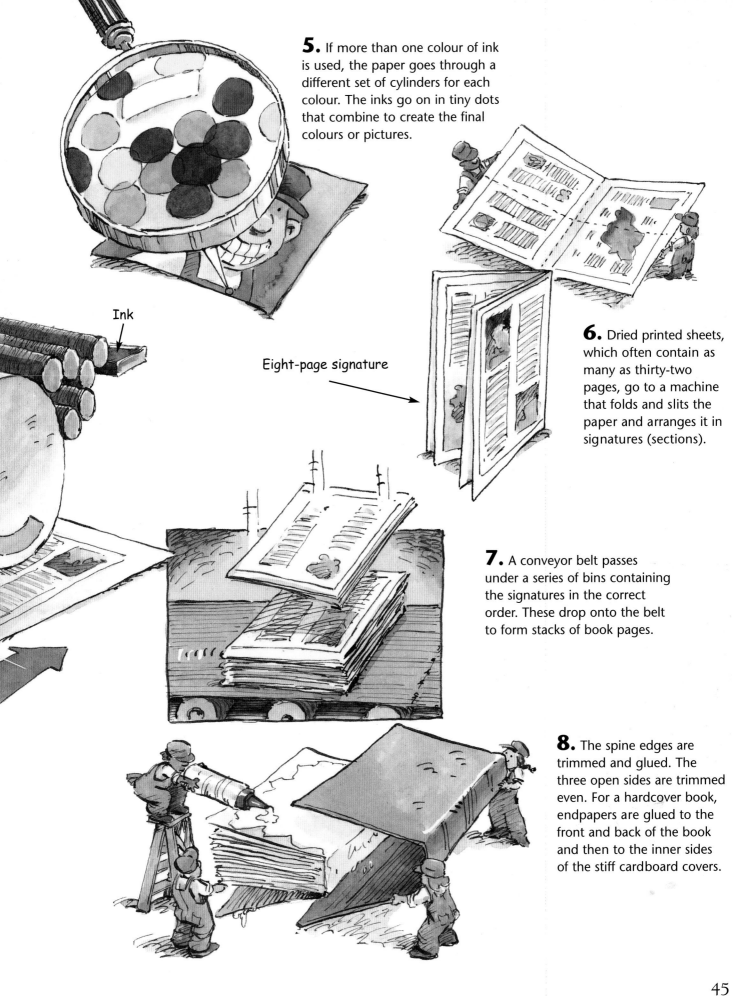

5. If more than one colour of ink is used, the paper goes through a different set of cylinders for each colour. The inks go on in tiny dots that combine to create the final colours or pictures.

Ink

Eight-page signature

6. Dried printed sheets, which often contain as many as thirty-two pages, go to a machine that folds and slits the paper and arranges it in signatures (sections).

7. A conveyor belt passes under a series of bins containing the signatures in the correct order. These drop onto the belt to form stacks of book pages.

8. The spine edges are trimmed and glued. The three open sides are trimmed even. For a hardcover book, endpapers are glued to the front and back of the book and then to the inner sides of the stiff cardboard covers.

45

Cat Litter

Until 1948, most cats used the great outdoors as their litter box, while a lucky few got indoor cat boxes filled with sand. But that winter, Kay Draper, a housewife in Michigan, USA, discovered that her sand pile had frozen solid. Luckily, the company next door sold pellets of a dried clay product called fuller's earth, used for soaking up spilt oil and petrol.

Mrs Draper borrowed a few cups of the clay and found it worked very well in her cat box. She came back for more, told her friends, and soon Ed Lowe (the company owner's son) began selling it in paper bags marked 'kitty litter'. And the rest is cat history.

Clay layer

1. Earth-movers scoop clay from open pits and place it on conveyor belts, which carry it to a crusher to be broken into smaller chunks.

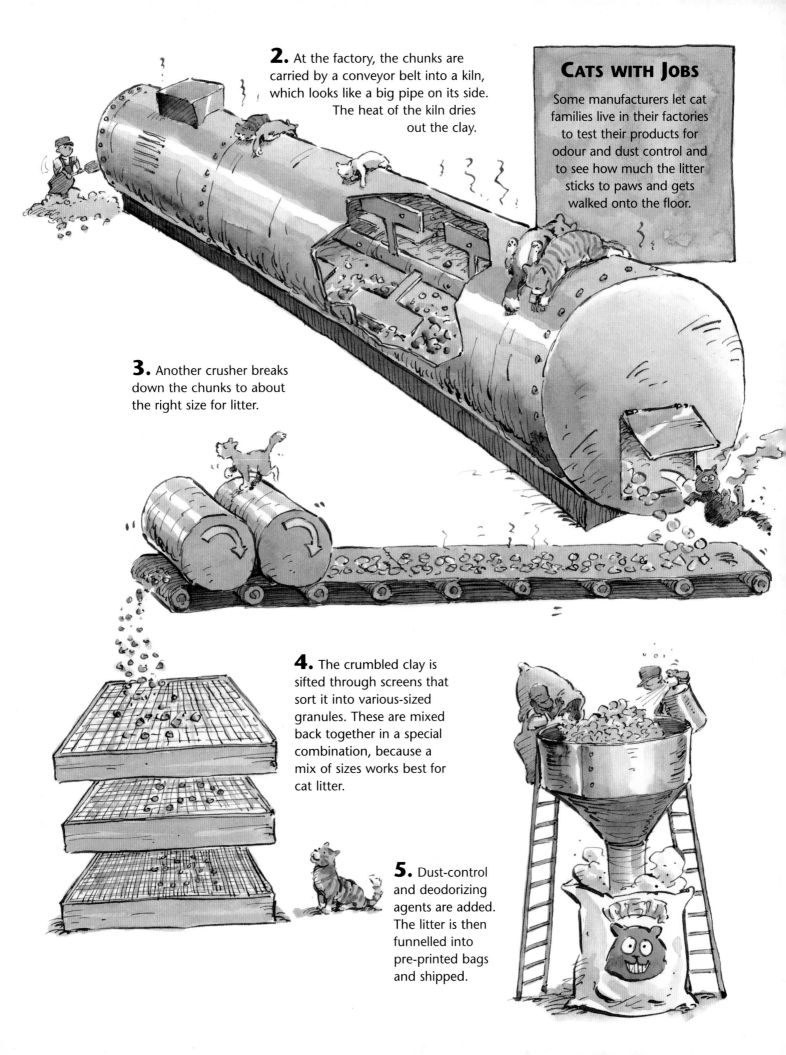

2. At the factory, the chunks are carried by a conveyor belt into a kiln, which looks like a big pipe on its side. The heat of the kiln dries out the clay.

CATS WITH JOBS

Some manufacturers let cat families live in their factories to test their products for odour and dust control and to see how much the litter sticks to paws and gets walked onto the floor.

3. Another crusher breaks down the chunks to about the right size for litter.

4. The crumbled clay is sifted through screens that sort it into various-sized granules. These are mixed back together in a special combination, because a mix of sizes works best for cat litter.

5. Dust-control and deodorizing agents are added. The litter is then funnelled into pre-printed bags and shipped.

Crayons

If you had bought a box of crayons in 1900, black would have been your favourite colour, because that was the *only* colour. Crayons were used mainly in factories and on farms as waterproof markers. It was not long before artists had coloured crayons to work with, but they were toxic and therefore dangerous for children to use.

In 1903, an American company named Binney and Smith came up with coloured crayons that were safe for kids and so were suitable for use in schools. Today, the company makes more than 2 billion Crayola brand crayons a year.

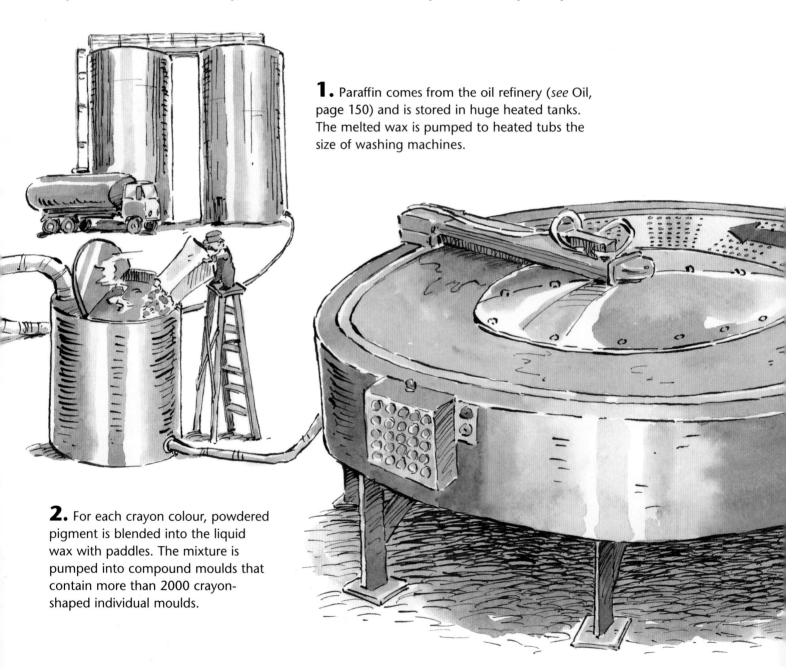

1. Paraffin comes from the oil refinery (*see* Oil, page 150) and is stored in huge heated tanks. The melted wax is pumped to heated tubs the size of washing machines.

2. For each crayon colour, powdered pigment is blended into the liquid wax with paddles. The mixture is pumped into compound moulds that contain more than 2000 crayon-shaped individual moulds.

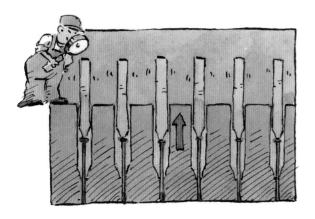

4. Metal rods push the crayons out of the moulds and into an inspection bin, where they are checked for breaks or other imperfections.

GET SOME GLITZ!

'Glitter' crayons have bits of shiny, reflective material mixed in with the wax and pigment.

3. Cool water circulates around each mould. Some colours take longer than others to harden, but in four to seven minutes all have set.

5. Each crayon is mechanically double-wrapped in paper for strength. The colour and brand names have been pre-printed on the side.

6. Different slots in the packing machine are filled, each with a different colour. Assortments of crayons are fed into cardboard sleeves, which are slid into boxes ready to be shipped.

49

Cutlery

It is the year 1066, and you are having dinner with William the Conqueror of England. You've brought your dagger, because guests are expected to supply their own eating utensils. You watch as the king tears off a big slab of roast beef, hacks it into pieces, and pops the bits into his mouth with his fingers. Are you shocked? Certainly not. Forks (and modern table manners) have yet to be invented.

Knives and spoons have been around pretty much forever, but forks did not really catch on in Europe until the 1400s. Here's how stainless-steel cutlery is made today.

1. Flat blanks in the shape of knives, forks and spoons are stamped out of sheets of stainless steel (*see* Iron and Steel, page 144).

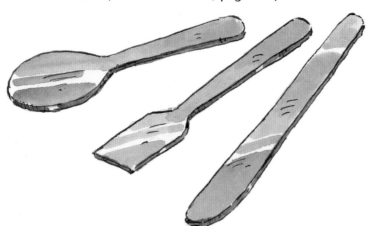

2. The blanks pass through a series of rollers to make each part the right thickness. For example, the handle of a spoon may be made thicker for strength and comfort. During this process, the blanks are heated to very high temperatures. This process, called annealing, makes the steel pliable.

Thin

Thick

3. Each piece is trimmed to size in a cut-out press, and the trimmings go back to be melted and reused. The prongs of a fork are cut out at this stage, with a narrow strip of metal left across the tip of the prongs to be removed later.

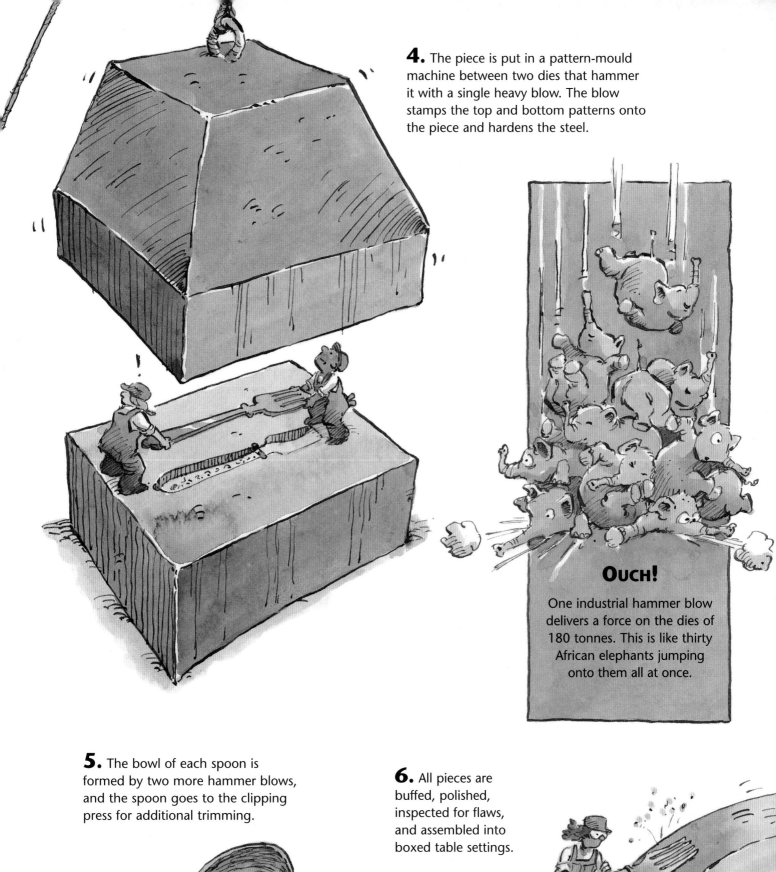

4. The piece is put in a pattern-mould machine between two dies that hammer it with a single heavy blow. The blow stamps the top and bottom patterns onto the piece and hardens the steel.

OUCH!

One industrial hammer blow delivers a force on the dies of 180 tonnes. This is like thirty African elephants jumping onto them all at once.

5. The bowl of each spoon is formed by two more hammer blows, and the spoon goes to the clipping press for additional trimming.

6. All pieces are buffed, polished, inspected for flaws, and assembled into boxed table settings.

51

Dental Floss

You lie flat on your back and helpless in the dentist's chair. The overhead light is blinding. The dentist leans over, looks in your mouth, and asks that question you've been dreading: 'Have you been flossing?'

As we all know, dental floss helps remove bits of food and plaque – that sticky stuff that hides between our teeth and attacks our gums. But cotton and other natural threads break easily. Manufacturers have had to come up with several new kinds of thread to loosen the gunk so you can brush it away.

So, have you been flossing?

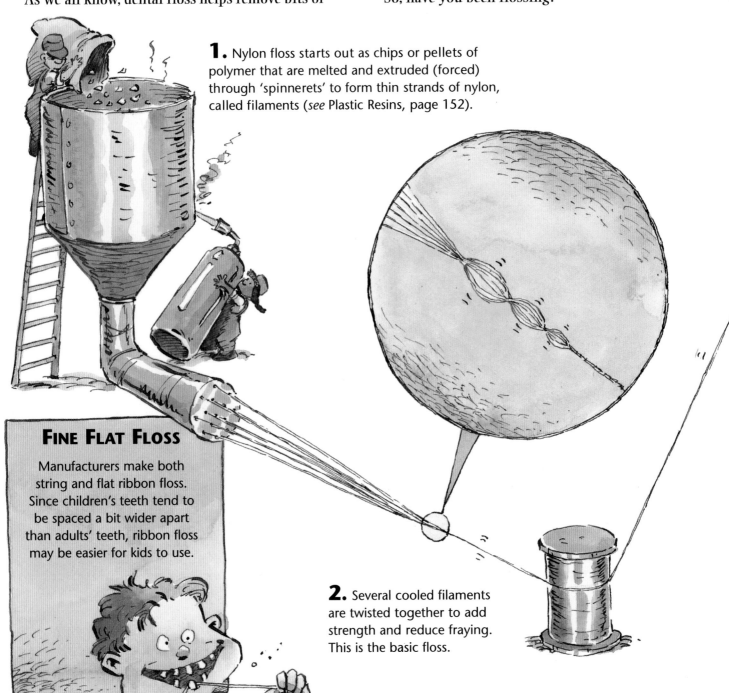

1. Nylon floss starts out as chips or pellets of polymer that are melted and extruded (forced) through 'spinnerets' to form thin strands of nylon, called filaments (*see* Plastic Resins, page 152).

FINE FLAT FLOSS

Manufacturers make both string and flat ribbon floss. Since children's teeth tend to be spaced a bit wider apart than adults' teeth, ribbon floss may be easier for kids to use.

2. Several cooled filaments are twisted together to add strength and reduce fraying. This is the basic floss.

3. The floss is pulled through a bath to coat it with wax. Flavours may also be added before it is wound onto a bobbin.

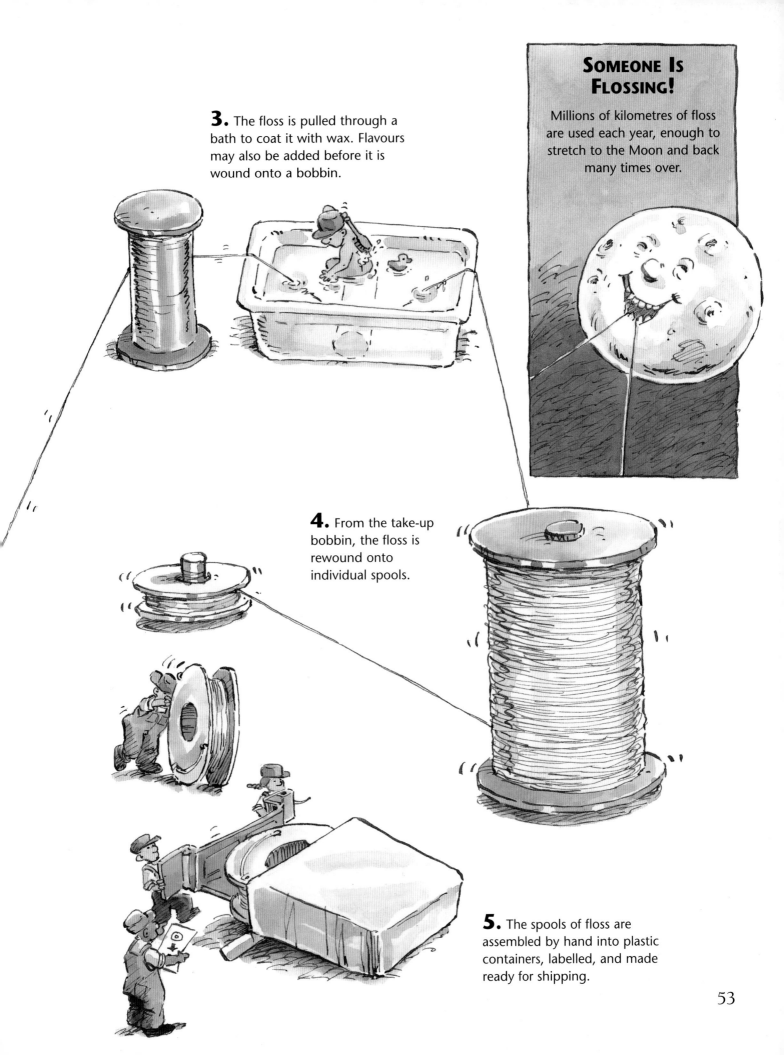

4. From the take-up bobbin, the floss is rewound onto individual spools.

5. The spools of floss are assembled by hand into plastic containers, labelled, and made ready for shipping.

Dry Pet Food

If your dog or cat did the shopping, would it pick tinned or dry food for its bowl? Of course, Rex and Ginger don't get to choose, although they may give you plenty of hints. Since about 1980, pet owners have been buying more and more dry products, such as kibble and biscuits. That's mainly because animal health experts have warned that too much soft food can lead to gum disease in pets.

Tinned or dry, pet food starts out much the same way.

1. A meat-processing factory renders meat by separating fat and water from the parts that contain protein. The dried protein then goes to the pet-food factory in large pieces, which are ground into smaller chunks.

2. Steamers cook the meat product. It is then ground further to a smooth texture.

3. Big mixers blend in other ingredients, including vitamins, soya beans, starches, flavours, and liquids such as water.

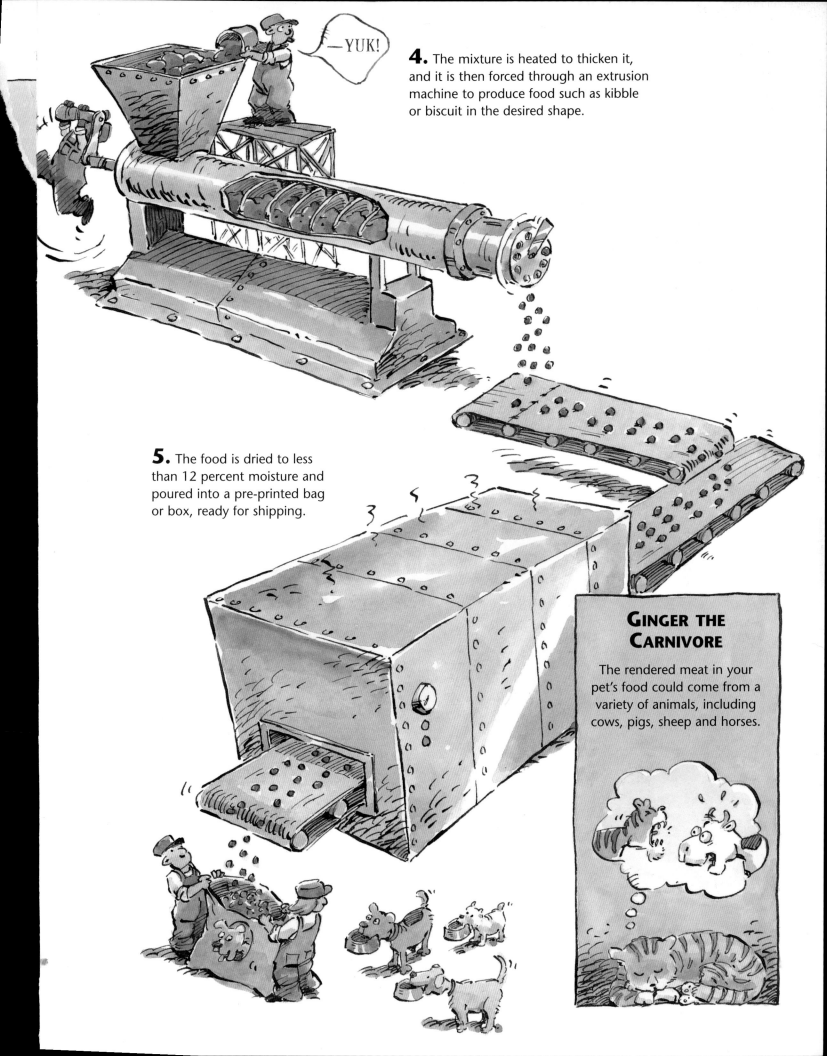

—YUK!

4. The mixture is heated to thicken it, and it is then forced through an extrusion machine to produce food such as kibble or biscuit in the desired shape.

5. The food is dried to less than 12 percent moisture and poured into a pre-printed bag or box, ready for shipping.

GINGER THE CARNIVORE

The rendered meat in your pet's food could come from a variety of animals, including cows, pigs, sheep and horses.

Rubbers

Europeans were using pencils back in the early 1600s (*see* Pencils, page 62). But if they needed to rub out an error, the best thing available was a piece of bread! Then in the 1700s, scientists got excited about the properties of a stretchy new substance from the Americas called caoutchouc.

An Englishman named Joseph Priestley suggested that a lump of the stuff was just the thing to rub away pencil marks. And so the rubber was born.

Today, delete keys may fix many of our mistakes, but we still need our pencils – and rubbers.

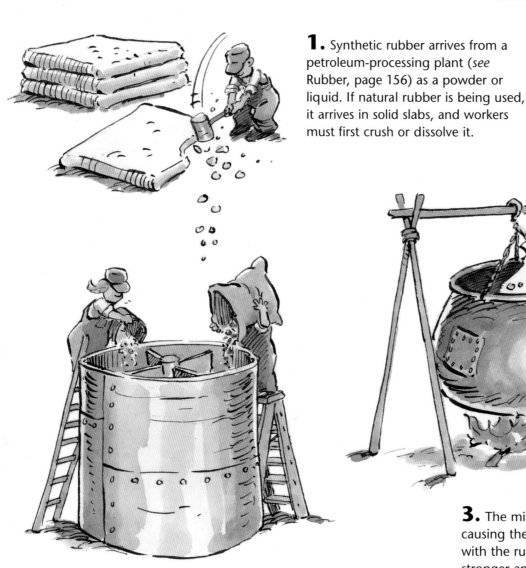

1. Synthetic rubber arrives from a petroleum-processing plant (*see* Rubber, page 156) as a powder or liquid. If natural rubber is being used, it arrives in solid slabs, and workers must first crush or dissolve it.

3. The mixture is heated, causing the sulphur to mix with the rubber and make it stronger and longer-lasting.

2. The rubber is mixed with ground pumice stone (to make it slightly gritty), iron oxide (to make it pink), vegetable oil, sulphur and other substances.

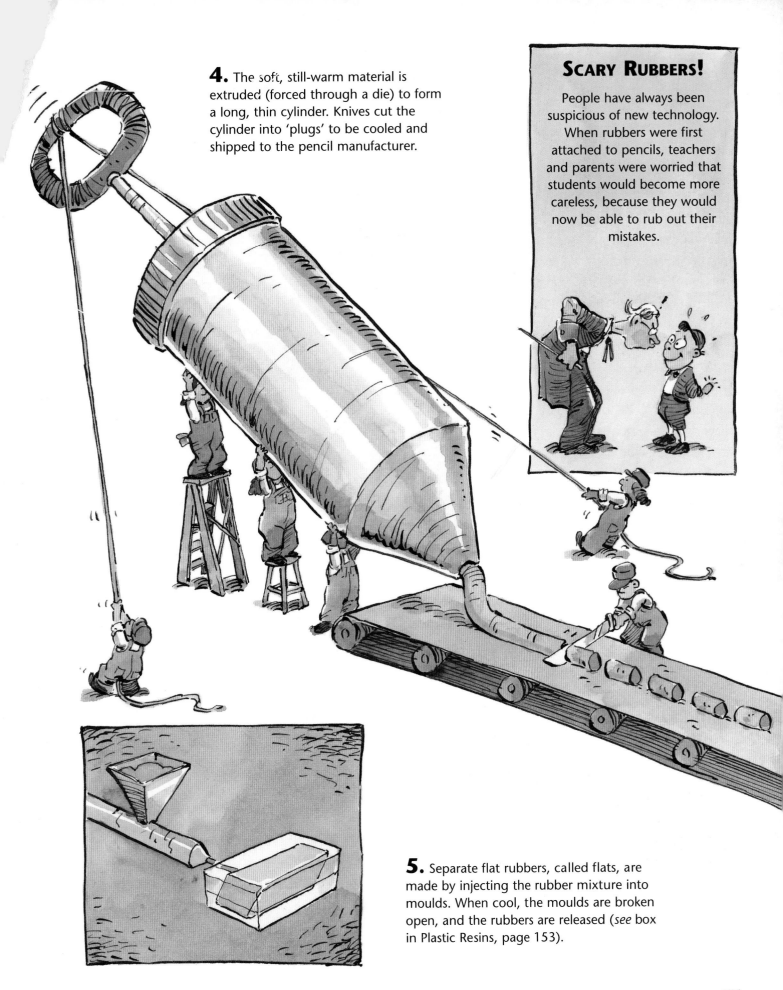

4. The soft, still-warm material is extruded (forced through a die) to form a long, thin cylinder. Knives cut the cylinder into 'plugs' to be cooled and shipped to the pencil manufacturer.

SCARY RUBBERS!

People have always been suspicious of new technology. When rubbers were first attached to pencils, teachers and parents were worried that students would become more careless, because they would now be able to rub out their mistakes.

5. Separate flat rubbers, called flats, are made by injecting the rubber mixture into moulds. When cool, the moulds are broken open, and the rubbers are released (*see* box in Plastic Resins, page 153).

Matches

'Don't play with matches' is a good rule to follow – unless you are a chemist like John Walker of England. In 1827, he and other inventors were looking for a quick, safe way to light a fire after it had gone out. Walker played around with different ideas and finally came up with matches. Unfortunately, they were hard to light.

'Strike-anywhere' matches tipped with yellow phosphorus appeared in Germany five years later. These were a little *too* easy to light and caused a lot of accidental fires. Besides, the yellow phosphorus made match-factory workers seriously ill. Then in 1855, red phosphorus 'safety' matches were produced in Sweden. These would light only when struck against a special surface and did not harm people's health.

1. Logs, usually pine or aspen, are stripped of their bark and cut into thin sheets called veneer.

4. The matches are guided onto a conveyor belt dotted with holding holes that keep the sticks upright. The belt passes upside down over a series of vats, coating the match ends.

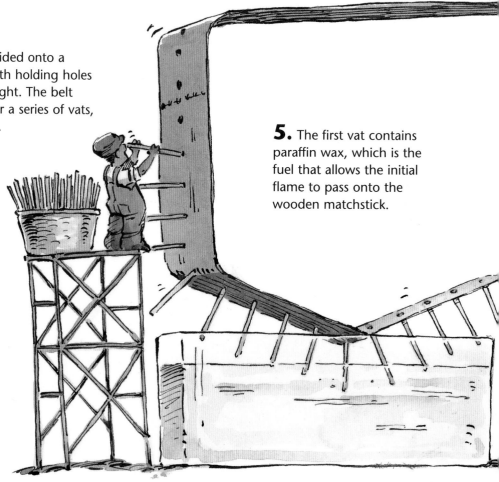

5. The first vat contains paraffin wax, which is the fuel that allows the initial flame to pass onto the wooden matchstick.

POOH!

Matches smell funny when they burn because they contain chemicals such as sulphur, animal glues, rosin and dyes to colour the match heads.

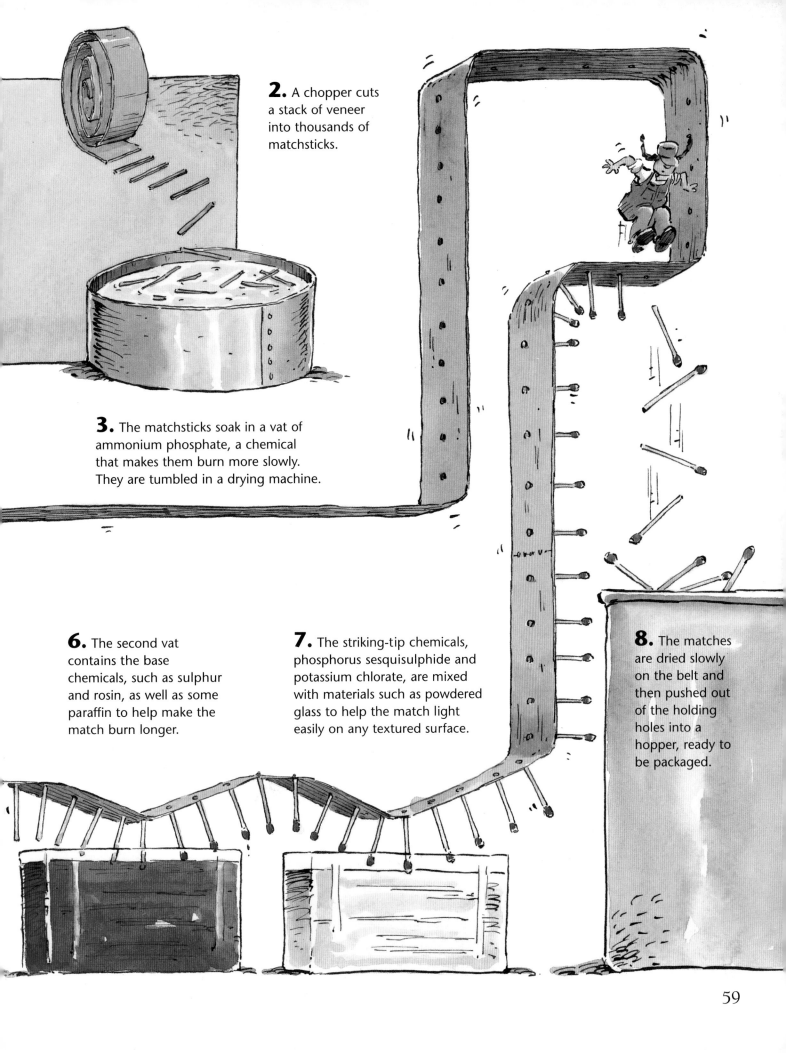

2. A chopper cuts a stack of veneer into thousands of matchsticks.

3. The matchsticks soak in a vat of ammonium phosphate, a chemical that makes them burn more slowly. They are tumbled in a drying machine.

6. The second vat contains the base chemicals, such as sulphur and rosin, as well as some paraffin to help make the match burn longer.

7. The striking-tip chemicals, phosphorus sesquisulphide and potassium chlorate, are mixed with materials such as powdered glass to help the match light easily on any textured surface.

8. The matches are dried slowly on the belt and then pushed out of the holding holes into a hopper, ready to be packaged.

Mirrors

Mirrors do more than help us comb our hair. The mirrors in microscopes let us look at germs and other things too small to be seen with the naked eye. And the mirrors in reflecting telescopes bring us closer to the stars and planets of outer space.

A mirror is any smooth surface with a shiny, dark background. Early mirrors were polished metal, but the invention of glass made better-reflecting mirrors cheap and easy to produce. The thin metallic backing, often silver, creates the mirror effect.

Modern mirror-making uses a continuous conveyor method.

WARPED

In the 1600s, mirror-makers began using silver to coat the backs. But early glass was often warped and rippled, creating 'fun house' images that would not have reflected kindly on viewers.

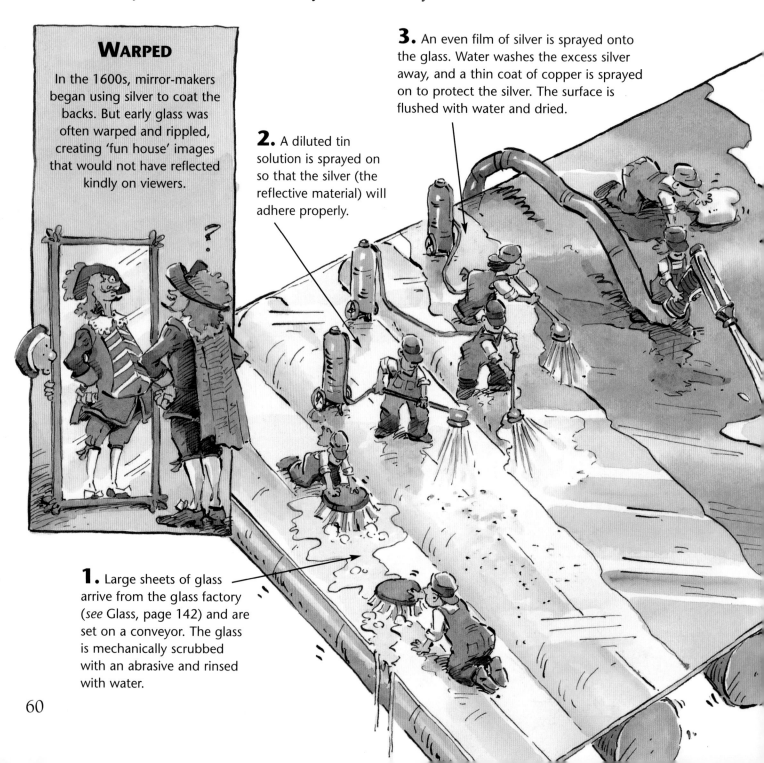

2. A diluted tin solution is sprayed on so that the silver (the reflective material) will adhere properly.

3. An even film of silver is sprayed onto the glass. Water washes the excess silver away, and a thin coat of copper is sprayed on to protect the silver. The surface is flushed with water and dried.

1. Large sheets of glass arrive from the glass factory (*see* Glass, page 142) and are set on a conveyor. The glass is mechanically scrubbed with an abrasive and rinsed with water.

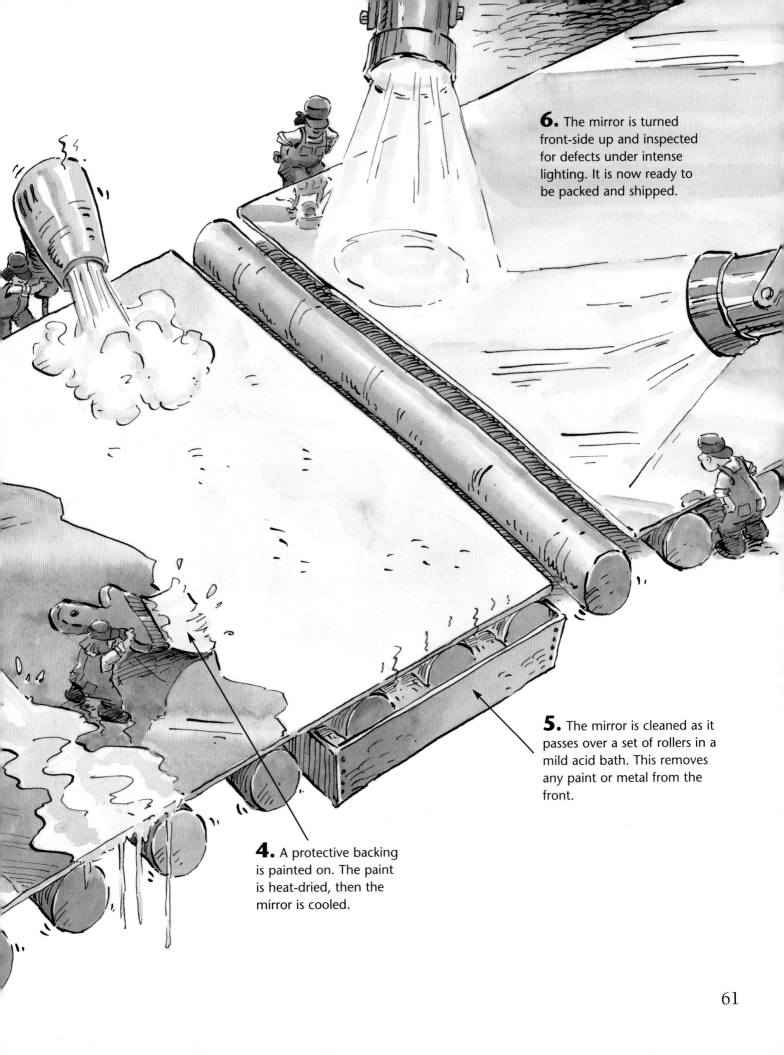

6. The mirror is turned front-side up and inspected for defects under intense lighting. It is now ready to be packed and shipped.

5. The mirror is cleaned as it passes over a set of rollers in a mild acid bath. This removes any paint or metal from the front.

4. A protective backing is painted on. The paint is heat-dried, then the mirror is cooled.

Pencils

*T*he first marking tool was probably a charred stick used to draw pictures on a cave wall. The early Greeks and Romans used pieces of lead. Then around 1564, miners near Borrowdale in northwestern England found a soft, shiny substance that made much darker marks than lead. They called it 'black lead'. Cut into thin sticks and wrapped with heavy string, the material made excellent markers.

Then in 1779, scientists discovered that black lead wasn't lead after all. It belonged to the pure natural carbon family of coal and diamonds, so they renamed it graphite. But most of us still call it lead.

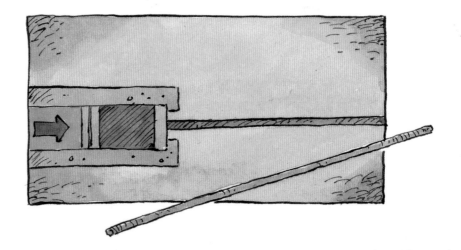

1. Graphite is powdered and mixed with clay, water, wax, and various other materials.

LEAD GRADES

The more graphite there is in a pencil lead, the softer it is. More clay makes the lead harder. Pencils marked 4B are extra soft, 4H means extra hard. HB pencils are in the middle and are suitable for most writing jobs.

2. The graphite paste is extruded (forced) through a narrow opening to create a thin rope. The rope is cut to pencil lengths and dried straight.

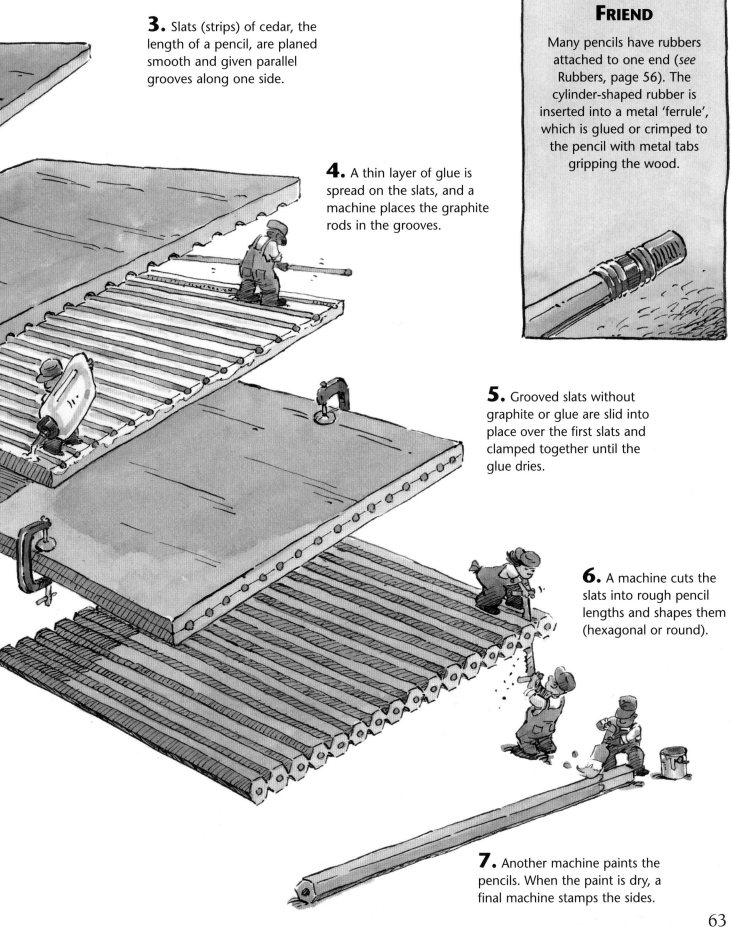

3. Slats (strips) of cedar, the length of a pencil, are planed smooth and given parallel grooves along one side.

4. A thin layer of glue is spread on the slats, and a machine places the graphite rods in the grooves.

THE WRITER'S FRIEND

Many pencils have rubbers attached to one end (*see* Rubbers, page 56). The cylinder-shaped rubber is inserted into a metal 'ferrule', which is glued or crimped to the pencil with metal tabs gripping the wood.

5. Grooved slats without graphite or glue are slid into place over the first slats and clamped together until the glue dries.

6. A machine cuts the slats into rough pencil lengths and shapes them (hexagonal or round).

7. Another machine paints the pencils. When the paint is dry, a final machine stamps the sides.

63

Cling Film

Transparent, non-waterproof 'cellophane' was invented in 1908 by a Swiss chemist named Jacques Brandenberger. This expensive early version of cling film was used mainly to package luxury items. In 1927, a waterproofing method was discovered that turned cellophane into an affordable packaging material everyone could use.

British chemists discovered another plastic wrapping material, polythene (polyethylene), by accident in 1933. It was originally used as electrical insulation to protect people from shocks.

Polythene is one of several plastics used today to make various brands of cling film. In its different forms it is also used to make plastic bags, plastic sheeting, squeezy bottles, rubbish bins…

3. The bubble forms in a tall tower. As it reaches the top, the tower sides narrow, collapsing the bubble until it is flat. Rollers at the top continuously draw up the flattened plastic film.

1. Beads of polymer arrive from the polymerizing factory (*see* Plastic Resins, page 152).

2. These are melted and extruded (forced) through a circular die. Air is blown through the middle and sides of the die as the plastic comes out, forming a huge bubble.

4. The edges are trimmed to create a double sheet of film. This is wound onto another roller, which may hold many kilometres of plastic film.

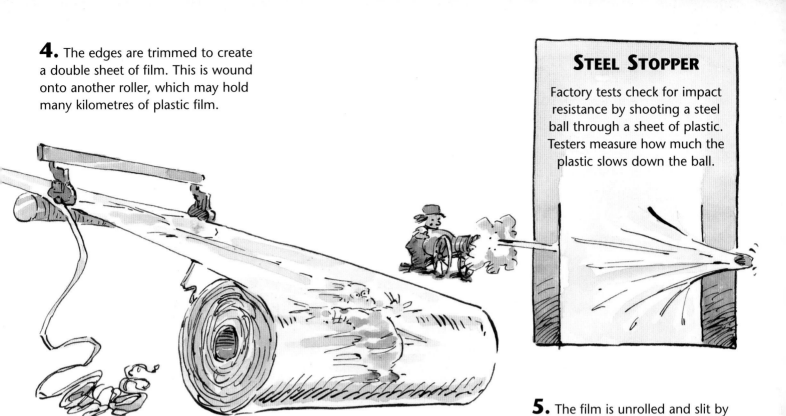

STEEL STOPPER

Factory tests check for impact resistance by shooting a steel ball through a sheet of plastic. Testers measure how much the plastic slows down the ball.

5. The film is unrolled and slit by machine to the desired length and width, usually about 20 m (66 ft) long by 35 cm (14 in) wide.

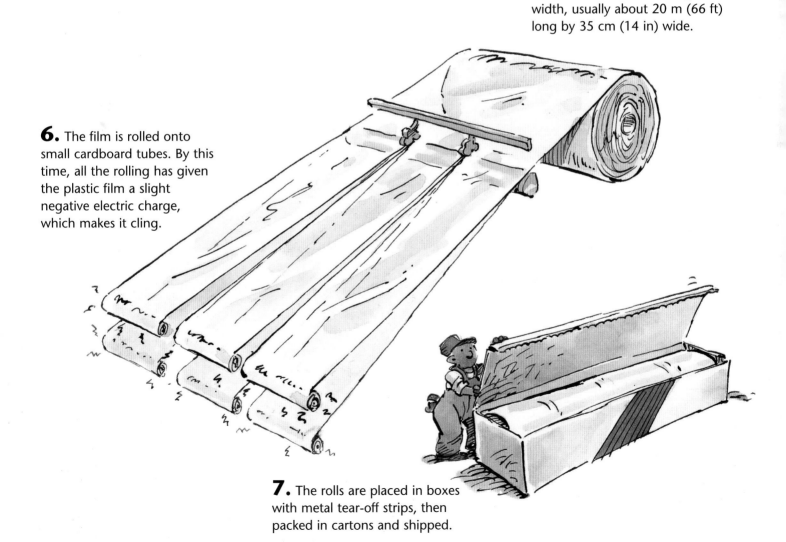

6. The film is rolled onto small cardboard tubes. By this time, all the rolling has given the plastic film a slight negative electric charge, which makes it cling.

7. The rolls are placed in boxes with metal tear-off strips, then packed in cartons and shipped.

Pottery

*I*t might have happened this way. One day thousands of years ago, someone was collecting grain in a wicker basket, but the seeds kept falling through the cracks. So she smeared the inside with some wet clay from a nearby stream and let it dry hard in the sun. That worked better, so everybody started doing it – until the day one of those baskets fell into a fire. The wicker burned away, leaving a much stronger clay pot.

Manufactured pottery production began in England in the early 1700s. Slip casting is one early method still used today.

1. Clay, water and other ingredients such as talc are mixed with big paddles in a large barrel-shaped 'blunger'.

2. The liquid 'slip clay' is poured into an absorbent mould. Some shapes need moulds made of two or more pieces that lock together and are wrapped with elastic bands.

3. As water is absorbed from the slip clay, a thin layer of clay forms on the inner surface of the mould. When this layer reaches the desired thickness, the still-liquid centre is poured out.

4. As the clay dries and hardens, it shrinks away from the sides of the mould. The mould is separated, and the seams on the raw pottery are scraped or sponged smooth.

5. For items such as teacups, the small handles are cast and attached separately.

6. Next is the kiln (furnace). One type, called a tunnel kiln, is 61 m (200 ft) long. Trolleys loaded with pottery roll in the warming end, through a very hot fire, and out through the cooling end. This process takes seventy to ninety hours.

7. Fired pottery is brushed or sprayed with a glaze and allowed to dry.

8. The glazed ware is loaded into box-like 'saggers' and fired again. The fire turns the glaze into a colourful, glassy coating.

Soap

The French, Italians and Spanish have been bathing with soap for hundreds of years. But in England, most people had to make do with water and a good scrub until 1853. Before that year, soap was heavily taxed and too expensive for most people to buy. Tax collectors would even lock the lids of soap-boiling pans at night to stop people from secretly making soap while the tax officials were sleeping.

By the late 1800s, industrially manufactured soap was widely available. Today, soap companies use the 'continuous' process, developed around 1940.

3. The mixture is fed into a tank where impurities sink and settle at the bottom.

1. Natural fat (from animal or vegetable sources) is boiled with salty water and an alkali such as caustic soda to produce crude soap.

Fat

Salty water

Alkali

2. The crude soap is spun in a 'centrifuge' to remove water and glycerin, a by-product.

Glycerin

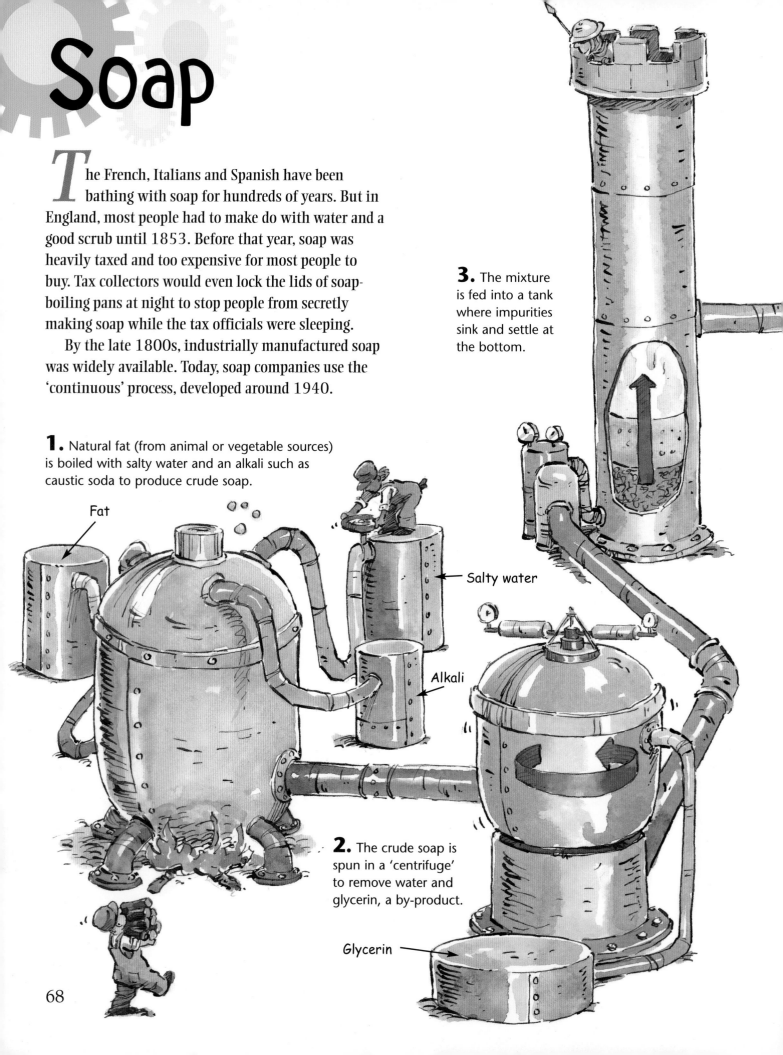

BOOM BOOM!

The leftover glycerin (step 2) isn't wasted. It is used for making two common products: hand lotion and dynamite.

4. The soap is dried by spraying it into a vacuum. It travels through a machine that reduces it to small lumps called noodles.

5. Fragrances and colours are mixed in, and the soap is extruded (forced through a die) into long bars, which are then cut into smaller pieces.

Phew, time for a bath!

6. The still-soft soap is cooled to firm it up, then stamped and pressed into its final shape before packaging.

69

Plasters

Before there were proper bandages, doctors would wrap wounds with cotton scraps swept up from factory floors. If you had an operation, you had a 50 percent chance of dying. No one knew then that the cause of infection in wounds was bacteria, invisible organisms in the air. A British surgeon named Joseph Lister figured that out in 1865. In 1876, a speech he gave in Philadelphia, USA, inspired Robert Johnson and his brothers to set up a company to manufacture cotton and gauze dressings sealed in germ-resistant packages.

In 1920, an employee of the Johnson & Johnson company thought of pre-sticking the sterilized gauze to a strip of surgical tape. This simple idea was a breakthrough because people with small wounds could now stick special bandages, or 'plasters', on themselves.

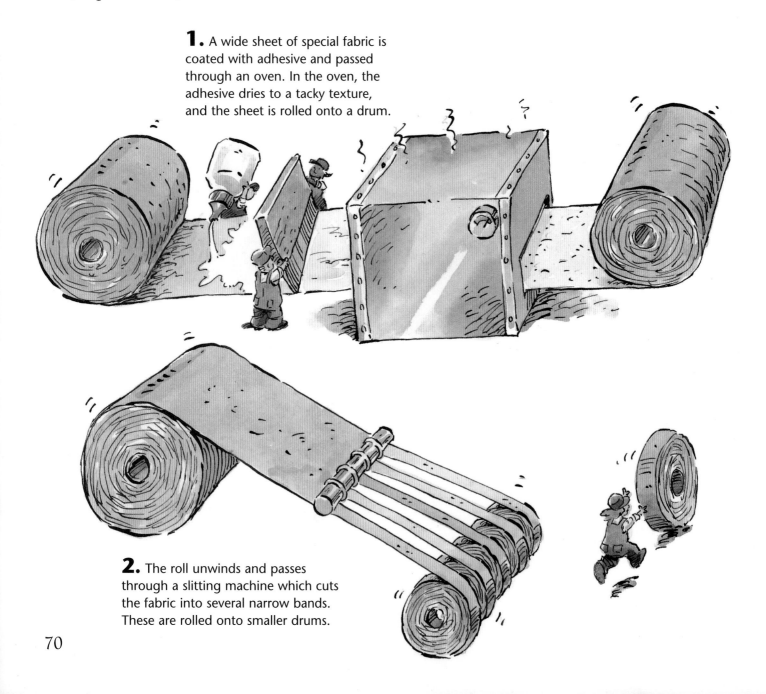

1. A wide sheet of special fabric is coated with adhesive and passed through an oven. In the oven, the adhesive dries to a tacky texture, and the sheet is rolled onto a drum.

2. The roll unwinds and passes through a slitting machine which cuts the fabric into several narrow bands. These are rolled onto smaller drums.

70

3. A strip of padded gauze is attached to the middle of each band of fabric as it is unrolled.

4. Two throwaway strips of plastic are laid on top. The band of fabric, gauze and plastic is then cut into separate plasters.

5. The individual plasters are placed between two strips of paper.

6. A perforating machine allows the individual plasters to be easily separated before they are packed in boxes.

7. Stacked boxes (about 500,000 plasters at once) go into a sterilizing chamber. Gas, heat and steam kill any germs, then the plasters are shipped off to stores.

MADE IN THE SHADE

Plasters come in a wide range of patterns and colours and in every skin shade – liquorice, mocha, coffee, cinnamon, honey, pink or white.

71

Toothpaste

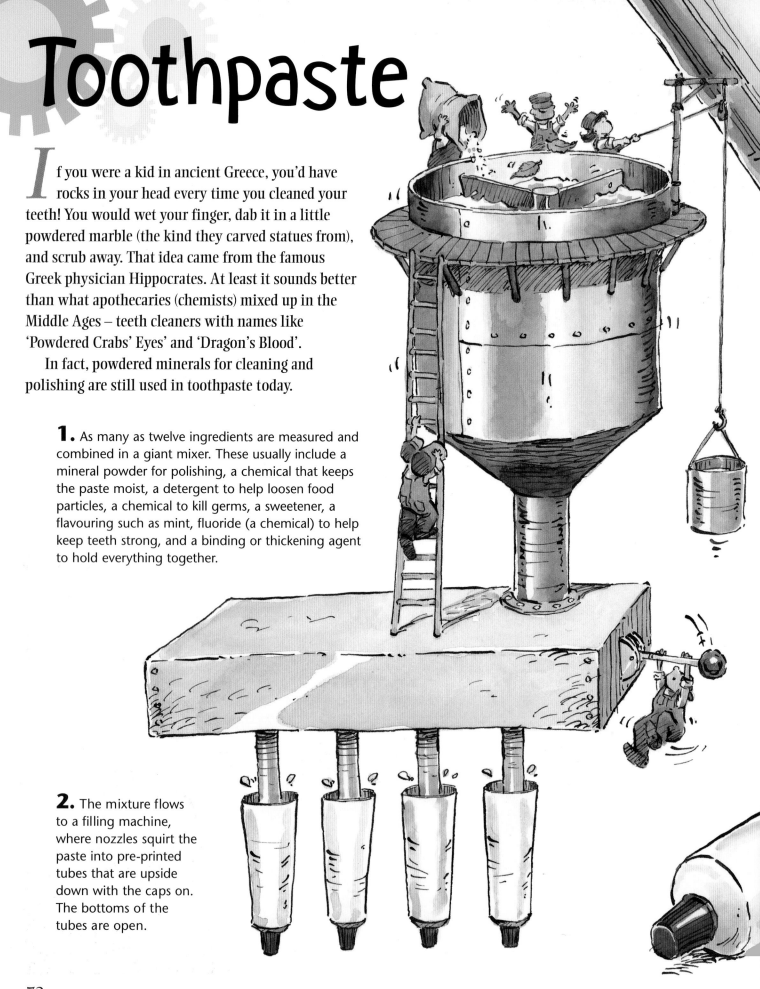

If you were a kid in ancient Greece, you'd have rocks in your head every time you cleaned your teeth! You would wet your finger, dab it in a little powdered marble (the kind they carved statues from), and scrub away. That idea came from the famous Greek physician Hippocrates. At least it sounds better than what apothecaries (chemists) mixed up in the Middle Ages – teeth cleaners with names like 'Powdered Crabs' Eyes' and 'Dragon's Blood'.

In fact, powdered minerals for cleaning and polishing are still used in toothpaste today.

1. As many as twelve ingredients are measured and combined in a giant mixer. These usually include a mineral powder for polishing, a chemical that keeps the paste moist, a detergent to help loosen food particles, a chemical to kill germs, a sweetener, a flavouring such as mint, fluoride (a chemical) to help keep teeth strong, and a binding or thickening agent to hold everything together.

2. The mixture flows to a filling machine, where nozzles squirt the paste into pre-printed tubes that are upside down with the caps on. The bottoms of the tubes are open.

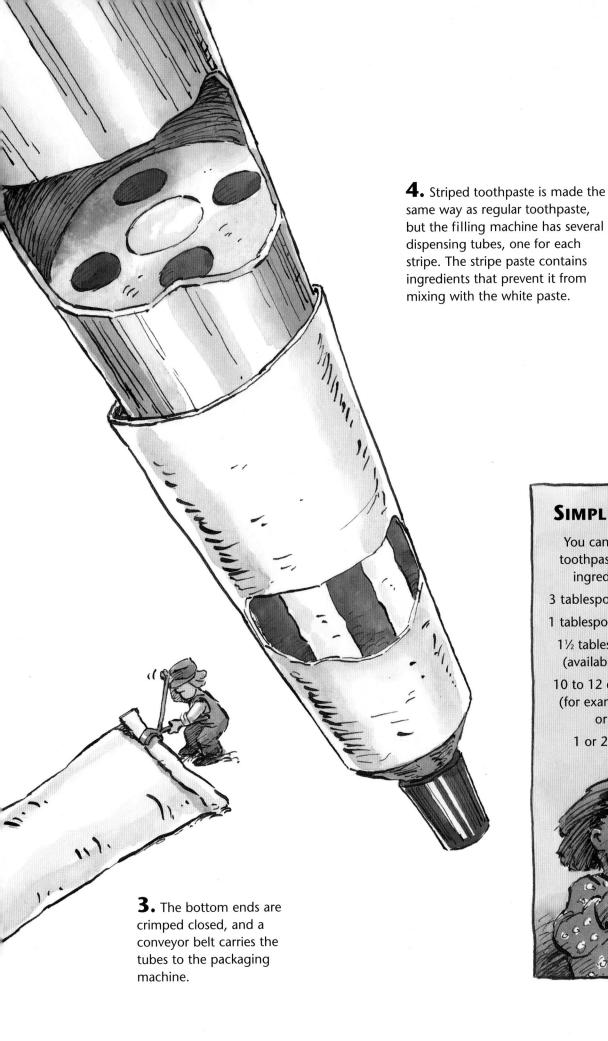

4. Striped toothpaste is made the same way as regular toothpaste, but the filling machine has several dispensing tubes, one for each stripe. The stripe paste contains ingredients that prevent it from mixing with the white paste.

SIMPLE BUT GOOD

You can make your own toothpaste. Just mix these ingredients together:

3 tablespoons of baking soda

1 tablespoon of fine-grain salt

1½ tablespoons of glycerin (available at pharmacies)

10 to 12 drops of flavouring (for example, peppermint or cinnamon)

1 or 2 drops of water

3. The bottom ends are crimped closed, and a conveyor belt carries the tubes to the packaging machine.

Candles

The first candles were probably sticks dipped in tallow (animal fat). Beeswax came later, smelt better, and made no mess because it burned instead of dripping. In the 1700s, the whaling trade introduced wax made from whale blubber, which stayed firm even in summer temperatures. In the 1860s, paraffin wax, made from oil (*see* Oil, page 150), became a popular choice and is still the most common material used for making candles.

Today, candles are made in a number of ways, including being pressed from powdered wax, formed in moulds or extruded by machines. The dipping process is still used as well, although machines have replaced much of the labour.

1. The wick is made from cotton or linen, braided and treated with chemicals to control how fast it burns.

Mind Your Beeswax

Beeswax is made, yes, by bees! They secrete it from glands in their bodies. Beekeepers remove the honey from the comb and melt the wax in boiling water. The wax rises to the surface and is skimmed off. It is then melted again and filtered to purify it further.

2. The wick winds off a spool and through a vat of paraffin. A large metal cooling drum hardens the wax as it passes over it and onto a spool.

3. A frame holding ninety-six wicks is prepared for the dipping machine.

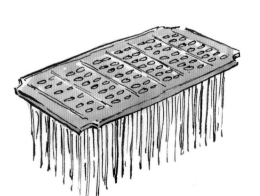

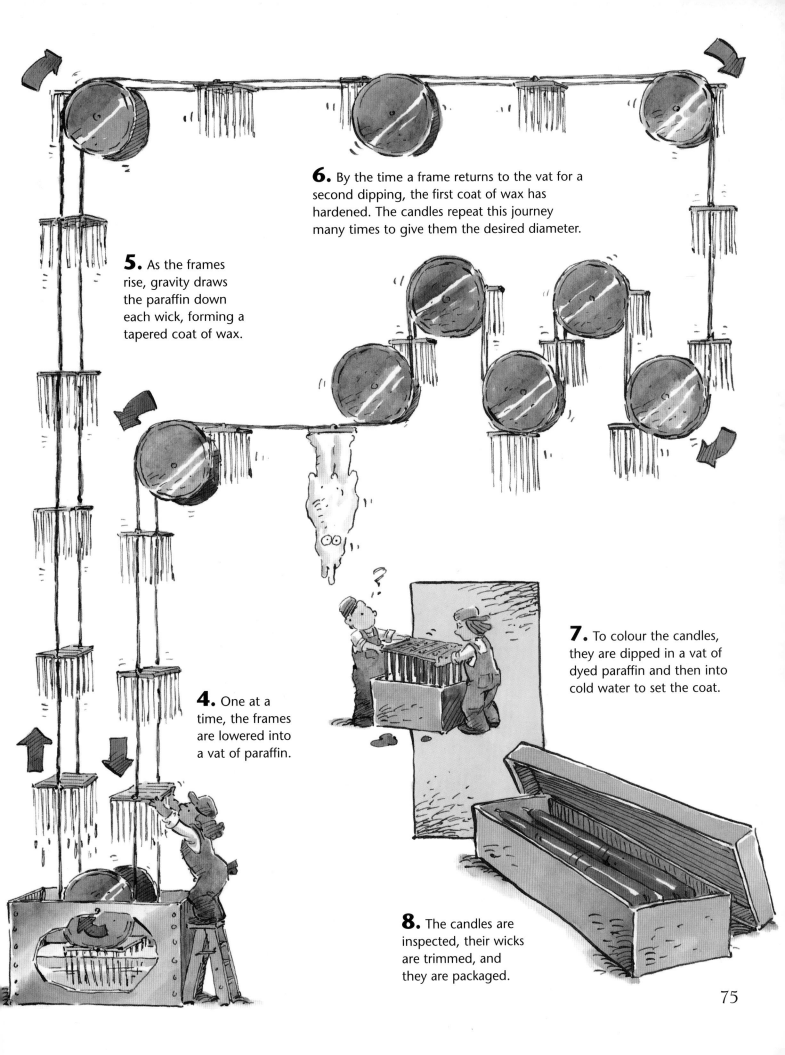

6. By the time a frame returns to the vat for a second dipping, the first coat of wax has hardened. The candles repeat this journey many times to give them the desired diameter.

5. As the frames rise, gravity draws the paraffin down each wick, forming a tapered coat of wax.

4. One at a time, the frames are lowered into a vat of paraffin.

7. To colour the candles, they are dipped in a vat of dyed paraffin and then into cold water to set the coat.

8. The candles are inspected, their wicks are trimmed, and they are packaged.

75

Wire

When you think of wire, you might remember that jumble of toaster, microwave, radio and coffeemaker wires competing for space at the back of the kitchen worktop. Other wires in your home actually hold it together – we call those screws and nails.

Some wires are hardly noticeable, such as the filaments inside lightbulbs. They're tiny yet strong enough to carry great amounts of electricity thousands of times before burning out. Other wires are thick cables – strands of wire twisted together. The thickest cables hold huge ships at anchor or suspend long bridges high in the air.

1. Small blocks of steel (*see* Iron and Steel, page 144) travel through a series of rollers. The rollers shape them into long bars and then rods about 6 mm (¼ in) in diameter.

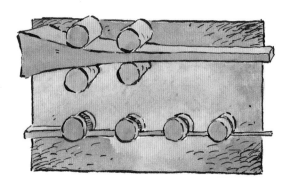

Lubricant

3. The end of the coil is sharpened and fed through a die (a funnel-shaped form made of very hard steel) which makes the wire thinner as it is pulled through.

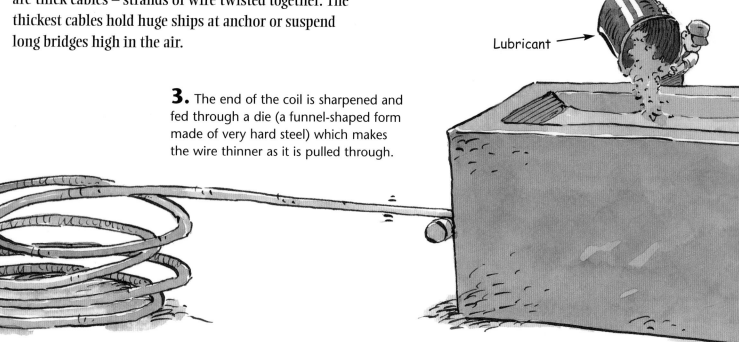

6. Wire often travels through a series of dies. Each die's opening is a little smaller than the previous one, narrowing the wire until it is the right size.

2. The rods are welded into long coils and soaked in a sulphuric-acid bath to remove the hard scale formed during the rolling process. The coil is then coated in a lime solution and baked to help carry the lubricant necessary when the wire is drawn (pulled).

Drum

4. As the point comes out of the die, pincers grab it and pull it onto a drum.

Die

5. A powerful engine turns the drum, drawing the wire through the die. The wire hardens as it is drawn, so heat is applied to keep it soft. Lubricants are also used throughout the process, and the die is water-cooled so that everything runs smoothly.

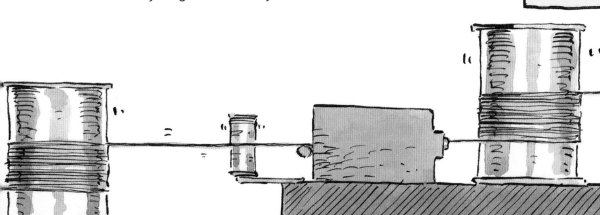

Soup to Nuts

Bread

The ancient Greeks and Romans made flour by having slaves or animals pull heavy stone rollers over grains and seeds. Bits of gravel, bones, ashes and whatever else was lying around the mill that day might also find their way into the baking. In those days, eating bread was an adventure!

Today, machines do most of the work of making bread. They even slice it.

1. Flour from the grain mill pours into a huge mixer. Water at the correct temperature, yeast, and other ingredients such as salt, honey, nuts and cracked grains are added.

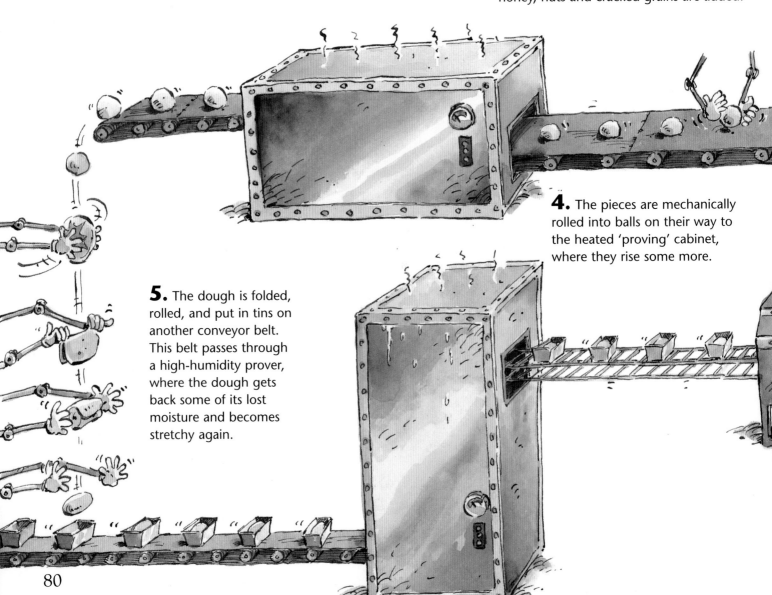

4. The pieces are mechanically rolled into balls on their way to the heated 'proving' cabinet, where they rise some more.

5. The dough is folded, rolled, and put in tins on another conveyor belt. This belt passes through a high-humidity prover, where the dough gets back some of its lost moisture and becomes stretchy again.

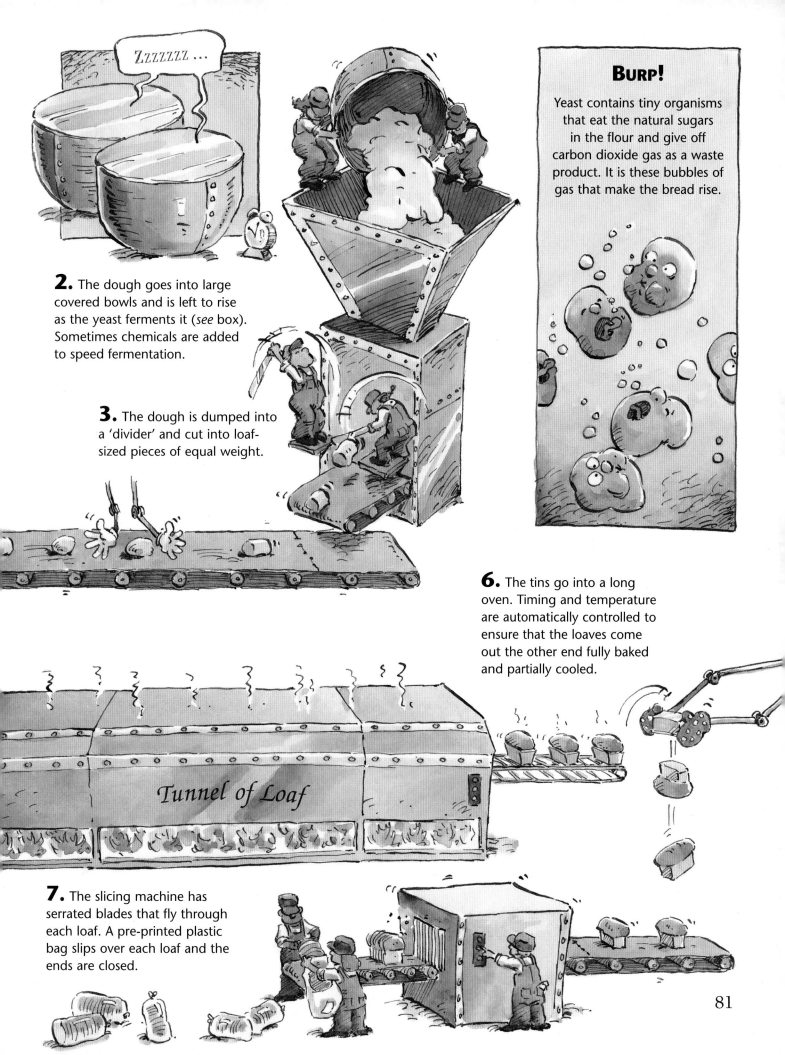

2. The dough goes into large covered bowls and is left to rise as the yeast ferments it (*see* box). Sometimes chemicals are added to speed fermentation.

3. The dough is dumped into a 'divider' and cut into loaf-sized pieces of equal weight.

Zzzzzzz ...

BURP!

Yeast contains tiny organisms that eat the natural sugars in the flour and give off carbon dioxide gas as a waste product. It is these bubbles of gas that make the bread rise.

6. The tins go into a long oven. Timing and temperature are automatically controlled to ensure that the loaves come out the other end fully baked and partially cooled.

Tunnel of Loaf

7. The slicing machine has serrated blades that fly through each loaf. A pre-printed plastic bag slips over each loaf and the ends are closed.

81

Cereal

If you want to know what cave people ate for breakfast, just grind up some oats, corn or wheat, then boil them in water and grab a spoon! If this sounds a lot like porridge, that's because it is. Today, most families prefer pre-cooked, ready-to-eat dry cereals, thanks to an American named John Harvey Kellogg. Interested in promoting a vegetarian diet, he and his brother, W. K. Kellogg, invented 'Granose' wheat flakes in 1894 and sold them in packages as health food. W. K. later started a cereal factory, creating a new industry.

This is how flaked cereals are made.

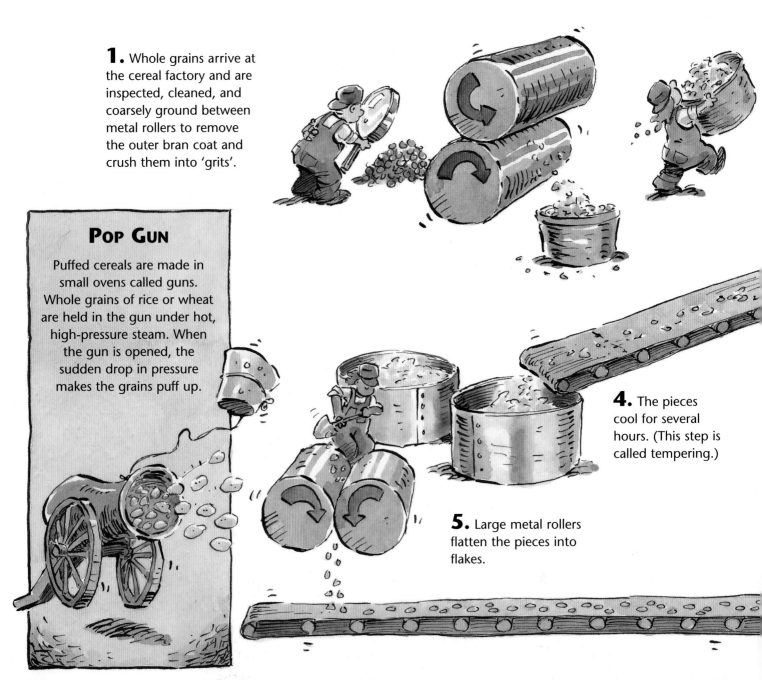

1. Whole grains arrive at the cereal factory and are inspected, cleaned, and coarsely ground between metal rollers to remove the outer bran coat and crush them into 'grits'.

POP GUN

Puffed cereals are made in small ovens called guns. Whole grains of rice or wheat are held in the gun under hot, high-pressure steam. When the gun is opened, the sudden drop in pressure makes the grains puff up.

4. The pieces cool for several hours. (This step is called tempering.)

5. Large metal rollers flatten the pieces into flakes.

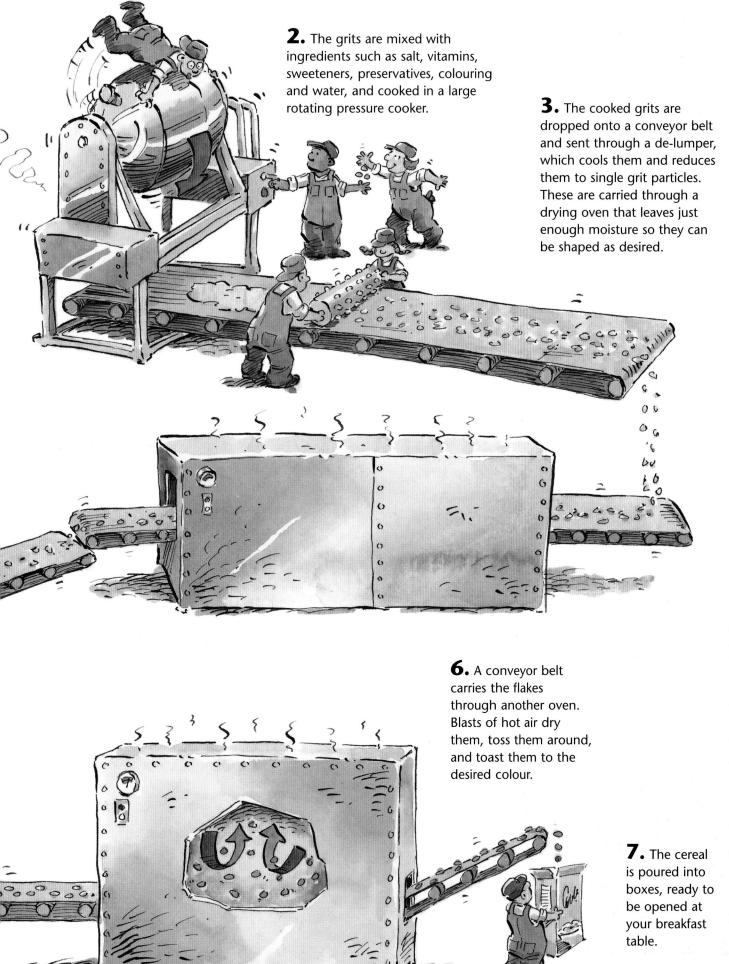

2. The grits are mixed with ingredients such as salt, vitamins, sweeteners, preservatives, colouring and water, and cooked in a large rotating pressure cooker.

3. The cooked grits are dropped onto a conveyor belt and sent through a de-lumper, which cools them and reduces them to single grit particles. These are carried through a drying oven that leaves just enough moisture so they can be shaped as desired.

6. A conveyor belt carries the flakes through another oven. Blasts of hot air dry them, toss them around, and toast them to the desired colour.

7. The cereal is poured into boxes, ready to be opened at your breakfast table.

Cheese

A sian nomadic people may have discovered cheese about 4000 years ago when the milk in their saddlebags (made of the lining of animals' stomachs) jiggled around in the hot sun. They found that cheese was much lighter to carry than milk, lasted longer and tasted delicious.

Cheese production spread to Europe and then, in 1611, to North America, when the first English cows walked off a sailing ship at Jamestown, Virginia.

Most cheese is made in factories today.

1. Fresh milk arrives in trucks and is pasteurized (*see* Milk, page 100) to remove harmful bacteria. It is then pumped into storage tanks.

2. When they are ready to make cheese, workers heat the milk in stainless-steel vats to between 30 and 36 °C (86–97 °F). They add starter culture – a liquid containing bacteria – which turns the milk sour. Vegetable dye (orange is common) may be added. Mechanical paddles stir the milk.

3. Rennet (a thickening agent) is mixed in, causing a soft rubbery substance called curd to form. Special knives cut the curd into small cubes, and watery whey starts to ooze out.

84

4. The curd is lifted out of the vat in a large 'dipping cloth' and hung up to let the whey drain away.

PACKED IN

To make a given quantity of cheese, you need more than ten times that much milk.

5. The curd forms a solid mass, which is packed into a circular metal mould for pressing. The press may be applied for a few hours or days, forcing out more whey.

6. The cheese is salted. (Some cheeses, such as cheddar, are salted before pressing.)

7. The round of cheese is sealed in plastic and cured (aged) in a warm room with controlled temperature and humidity for two months, a year or longer. Longer ageing sharpens the flavour.

8. The cheese is cut and repackaged in smaller sizes or shipped in big rounds, blocks, wedges, wheels or balls.

85

Chocolate

When Spanish explorers came to Central America in the 1500s, the Aztecs served them *cacahuatl*, a foamy drink made of cocoa beans, cornmeal, vanilla, red peppers and water. To Europeans, it tasted a lot better with sugar and other flavourings added, and the new drink gradually became a hit across Europe. By the 1700s, London's 'chocolate houses' were *the* places to be seen in.

Methods were later found to make solid chocolate, too. And in 1913, a Swiss confectioner named Jules Séchaud worked out how to get fillings into chocolates.

Chocolate starts with the cocoa tree, a delicate tropical evergreen.

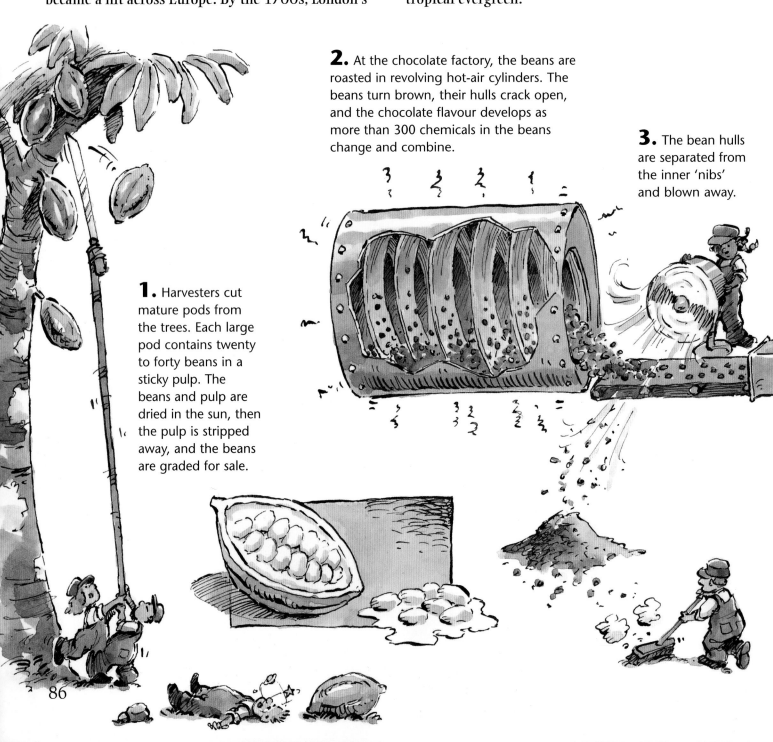

2. At the chocolate factory, the beans are roasted in revolving hot-air cylinders. The beans turn brown, their hulls crack open, and the chocolate flavour develops as more than 300 chemicals in the beans change and combine.

3. The bean hulls are separated from the inner 'nibs' and blown away.

1. Harvesters cut mature pods from the trees. Each large pod contains twenty to forty beans in a sticky pulp. The beans and pulp are dried in the sun, then the pulp is stripped away, and the beans are graded for sale.

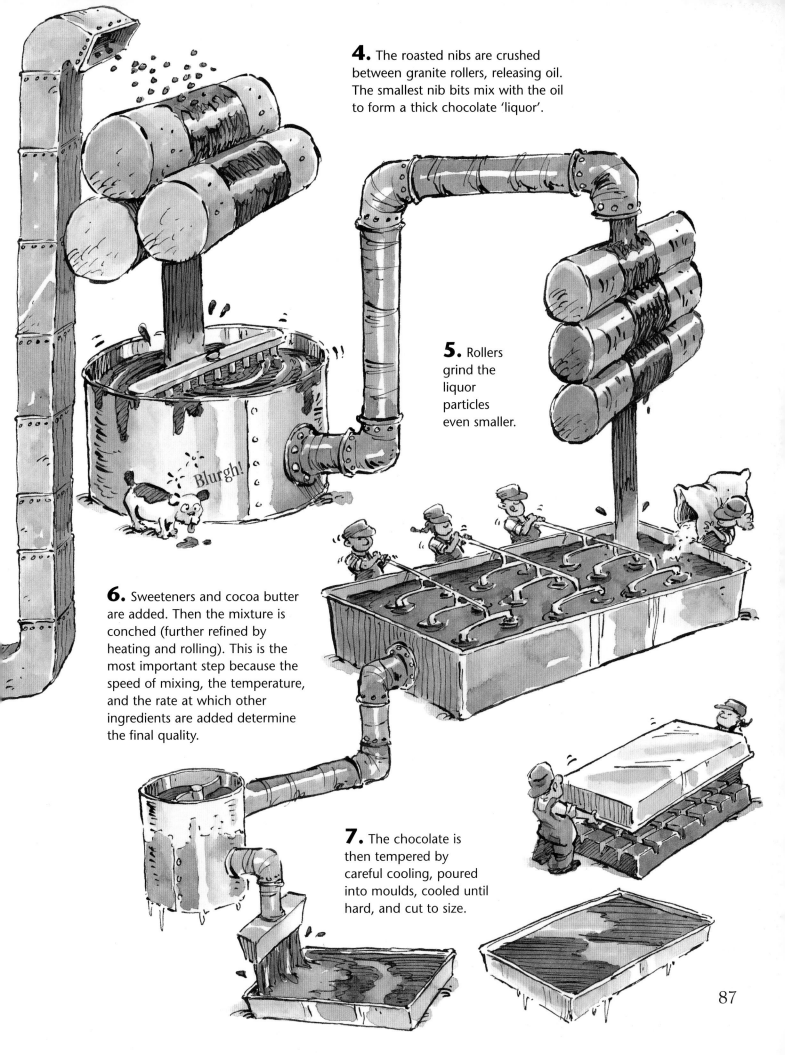

4. The roasted nibs are crushed between granite rollers, releasing oil. The smallest nib bits mix with the oil to form a thick chocolate 'liquor'.

5. Rollers grind the liquor particles even smaller.

6. Sweeteners and cocoa butter are added. Then the mixture is conched (further refined by heating and rolling). This is the most important step because the speed of mixing, the temperature, and the rate at which other ingredients are added determine the final quality.

7. The chocolate is then tempered by careful cooling, poured into moulds, cooled until hard, and cut to size.

Blurgh!

Cola

People have always believed in the curative powers of natural mineral water. First they only bathed in it. Then, in the late 1700s, they started drinking it. Soon after, chemists invented imitation mineral water by adding carbon dioxide gas to water to make it bubbly. In the United States, this drink was called soda water (soda makes fizz). Next came flavoured soda water, which was sold at soda fountains – shops where people gathered to socialize and enjoy the refreshing drinks. In 1886, John Pemberton of Atlanta, Georgia, created what is today the world's most famous drink, Coca-Cola. Early recipes contained caffeine (from the kola nut of a West African evergreen) and another stimulant from the leaves of the coca bush. Soon other cola companies sprang up offering their own versions. Today's colas are just as tasty, but not quite so zippy.

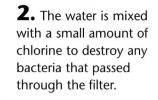
Kola nut

1. Regular drinking water is further purified with chemicals, causing any particles to clump together. These are removed by a filter.

2. The water is mixed with a small amount of chlorine to destroy any bacteria that passed through the filter.

3. A carbon filter removes the chlorine and other residues, as well as any dissolved air.

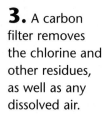

4. A syrup is made with sugar water and flavourings according to the manufacturer's secret cola recipe. This is sterilized using ultraviolet radiation or a fast heating-and-cooling pasteurization process (*see* Milk, page 100).

5. Machines mix the syrup and water in containers that are kept under pressure with carbon dioxide gas. This prevents air from getting into the mixture.

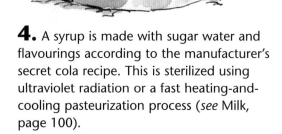
CENSORED

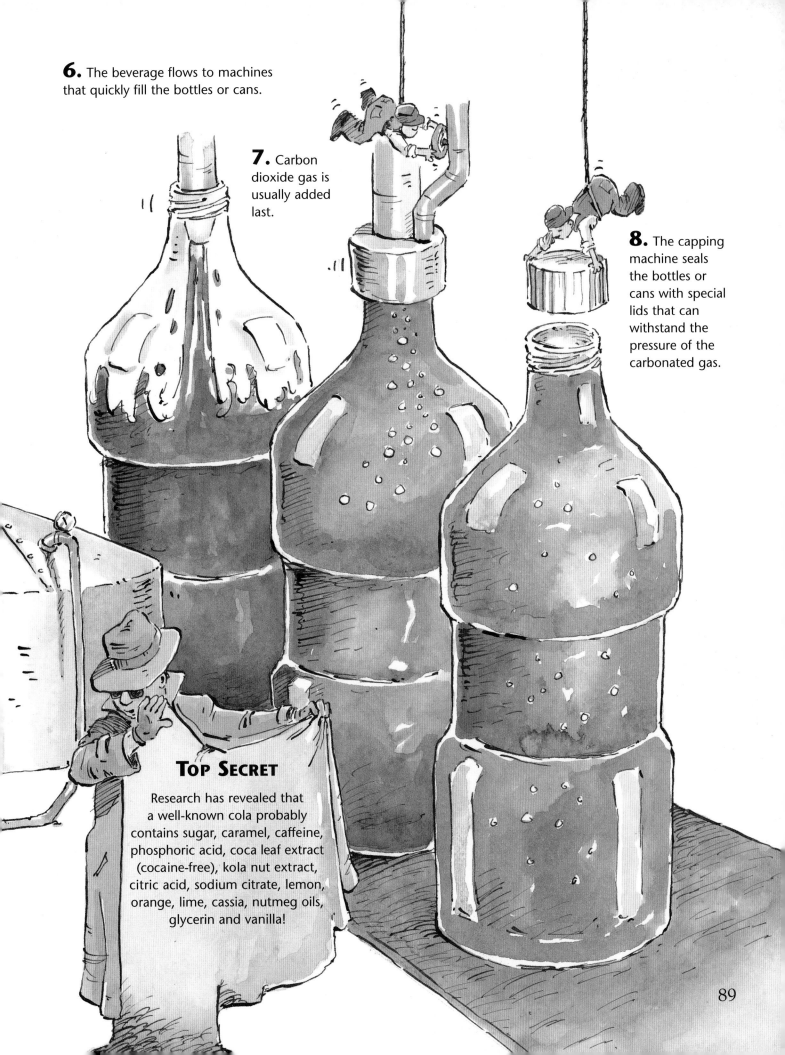

6. The beverage flows to machines that quickly fill the bottles or cans.

7. Carbon dioxide gas is usually added last.

8. The capping machine seals the bottles or cans with special lids that can withstand the pressure of the carbonated gas.

TOP SECRET

Research has revealed that a well-known cola probably contains sugar, caramel, caffeine, phosphoric acid, coca leaf extract (cocaine-free), kola nut extract, citric acid, sodium citrate, lemon, orange, lime, cassia, nutmeg oils, glycerin and vanilla!

Fortune Cookies

Nobody knows for sure where the idea of fortune cookies came from. One legend claims that in the 1300s, when China was under Mongol rule, the people planned a revolt by hiding messages in moon cakes. The foreign rulers didn't like moon cakes, so the plans went undetected and the rebellion succeeded, giving rise to the Ming Dynasty.

We do know that modern fortune cookies were invented in the United States (*see* box) and that the basic recipe includes flour, oil, sugar and eggs. But do the fortunes come true? Now, that's the real mystery.

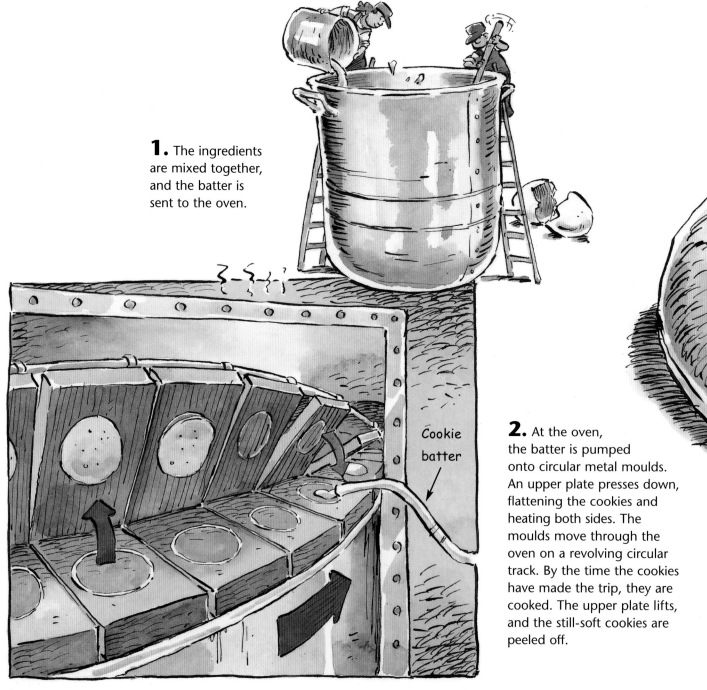

1. The ingredients are mixed together, and the batter is sent to the oven.

Cookie batter

2. At the oven, the batter is pumped onto circular metal moulds. An upper plate presses down, flattening the cookies and heating both sides. The moulds move through the oven on a revolving circular track. By the time the cookies have made the trip, they are cooked. The upper plate lifts, and the still-soft cookies are peeled off.

3. A pre-printed fortune is placed on each cookie, which is folded in half, making a D shape.

You will receive a fortune (cookie).

4. The top and bottom of the D are then pulled together, giving the cookie its characteristic shape.

5. The cookies are placed in a special holder to air-dry until they are hard and crisp.

Ice Cream

Real ice cream probably evolved in Europe in the 1600s. At first it was a dish for the rich, who had servants to do the hard work of mixing it. But that changed with the invention of the hand-cranked ice-cream churn in 1846. Then in 1851, a milk dealer in Baltimore, USA, named Jacob Fussell decided to make ice cream for sale and discovered there was more profit in it than in milk. Soon people were screaming for ice cream, and they haven't stopped since.

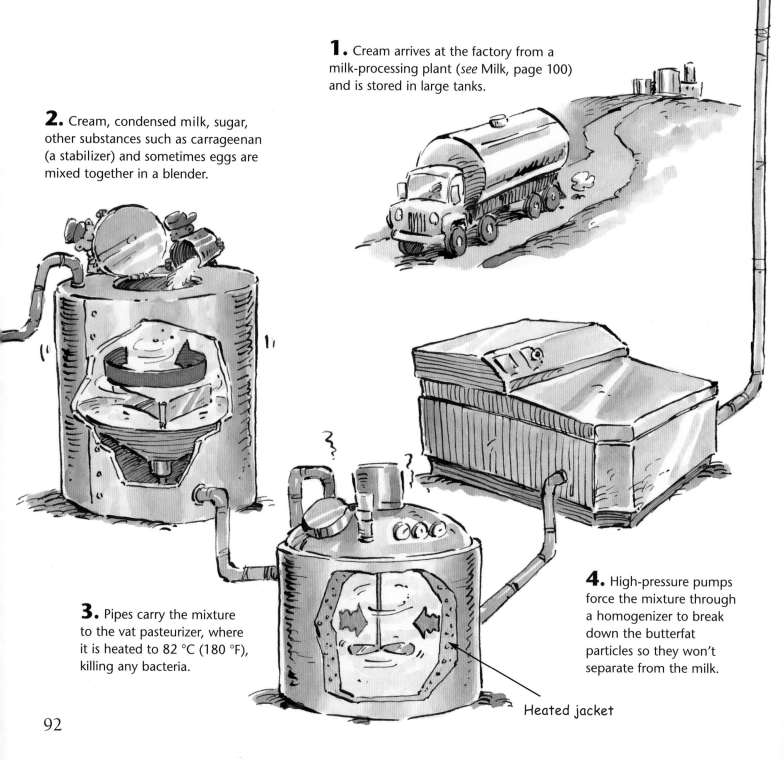

1. Cream arrives at the factory from a milk-processing plant (*see* Milk, page 100) and is stored in large tanks.

2. Cream, condensed milk, sugar, other substances such as carrageenan (a stabilizer) and sometimes eggs are mixed together in a blender.

3. Pipes carry the mixture to the vat pasteurizer, where it is heated to 82 °C (180 °F), killing any bacteria.

4. High-pressure pumps force the mixture through a homogenizer to break down the butterfat particles so they won't separate from the milk.

Heated jacket

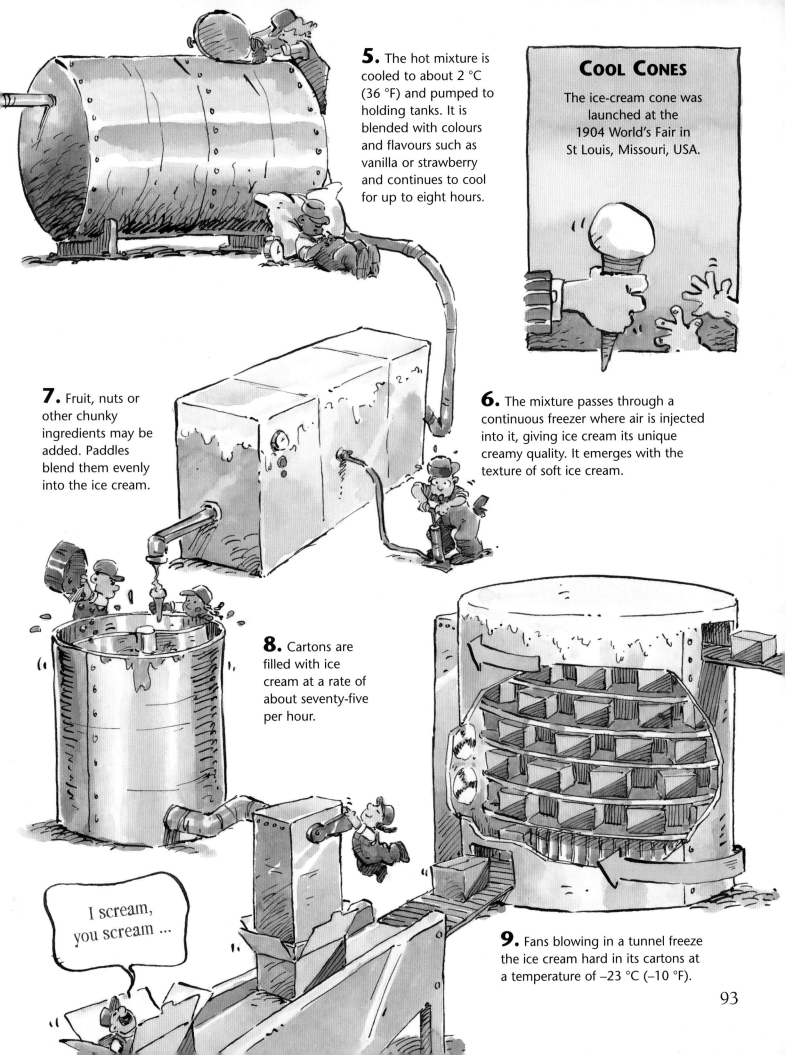

5. The hot mixture is cooled to about 2 °C (36 °F) and pumped to holding tanks. It is blended with colours and flavours such as vanilla or strawberry and continues to cool for up to eight hours.

COOL CONES

The ice-cream cone was launched at the 1904 World's Fair in St Louis, Missouri, USA.

7. Fruit, nuts or other chunky ingredients may be added. Paddles blend them evenly into the ice cream.

6. The mixture passes through a continuous freezer where air is injected into it, giving ice cream its unique creamy quality. It emerges with the texture of soft ice cream.

8. Cartons are filled with ice cream at a rate of about seventy-five per hour.

I scream, you scream ...

9. Fans blowing in a tunnel freeze the ice cream hard in its cartons at a temperature of –23 °C (–10 °F).

Jelly Beans

For hundreds of years, sweet lovers in the Middle East have made a chewy fruit-jelly confection called Turkish delight. Jelly beans combine the gummy centre with a hard outer shell, which was developed in France in the 1600s. Around 1900, the first traditional jelly bean flavours and colours appeared, such as sour lemon (yellow), cinnamon (red) and coconut (white).

Today's jelly bean lovers demand that their beans come in dozens of unusual flavours, such as bubble gum and watermelon (green outside, red inside).

1. Confectionery experts calculate the exact balance of ingredients and send the recipe to the sweet kitchen, where cooks mix up the sugary syrup for the centres. They also mix and cook the ingredients for the hard outer coating.

2. Cornstarch is packed into plastic trays, and then a machine presses bean-shaped dents into it. Each tray may have hundreds of dents.

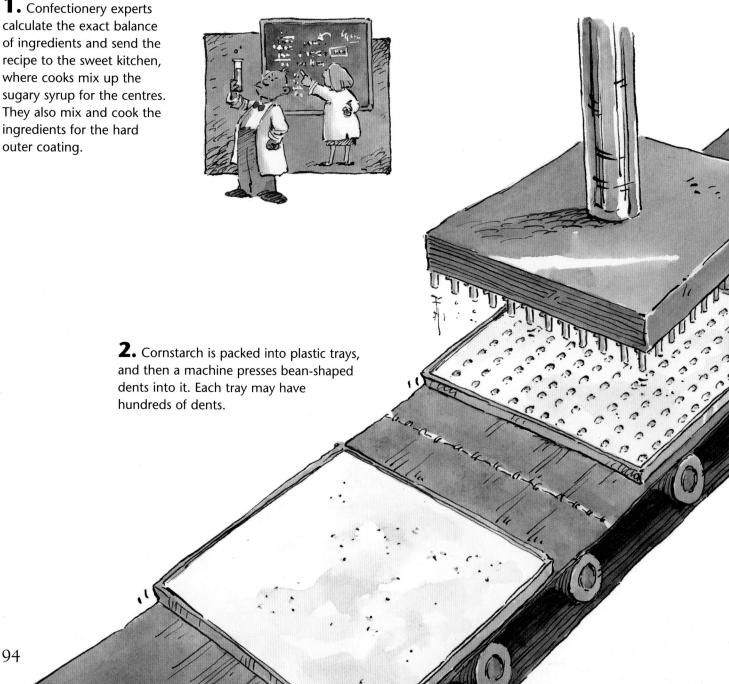

3. The trays are carried to the bean-casting area, where centre syrup is squirted in measured amounts into each dent. Then they go to the cooling room, where the centres cool down and harden.

4. After being coated in sugar so they don't stick together, the centres are dumped into rotating drums. Workers gradually add sugar, colours and flavours until a hard outer shell builds up and the beans reach the correct size. A confectioner's glaze is poured in to give the beans their glossy coat.

5. Several kinds of jelly beans are dumped into a mixing bin to create mixed lots. Beans that are too big or too small are filtered out, leaving only jelly beans of the right size. These get one more ride on a conveyor belt, where workers remove any imperfect beans.

THAT'S DISGUSTING!

Chemists have created all kinds of jelly bean flavours, including 'dirt' and 'earwax'.

Ketchup

Tomato ketchup started out as *ke-tsiap*, a Chinese sauce made from pickled fish or shellfish with no tomatoes in it at all. Europeans discovered *ke-tsiap* in the late 1600s, when English sea captains brought it home from their journeys to Malaysia and Singapore. English cooks brightened up the sauce with mushrooms, lemons and other ingredients, and by the 1800s, ketchup was a basic item on British tables.

But ketchup changed forever when cooks in the state of Maine, USA, started adding 'love apples' (the old name for tomatoes) to the homemade sauce. Then a man named Henry John Heinz turned it into a big business. In 1876, Heinz Tomato Ketchup hit the stores of America. Housewives snapped it up, happy to be free from the toil of making it themselves.

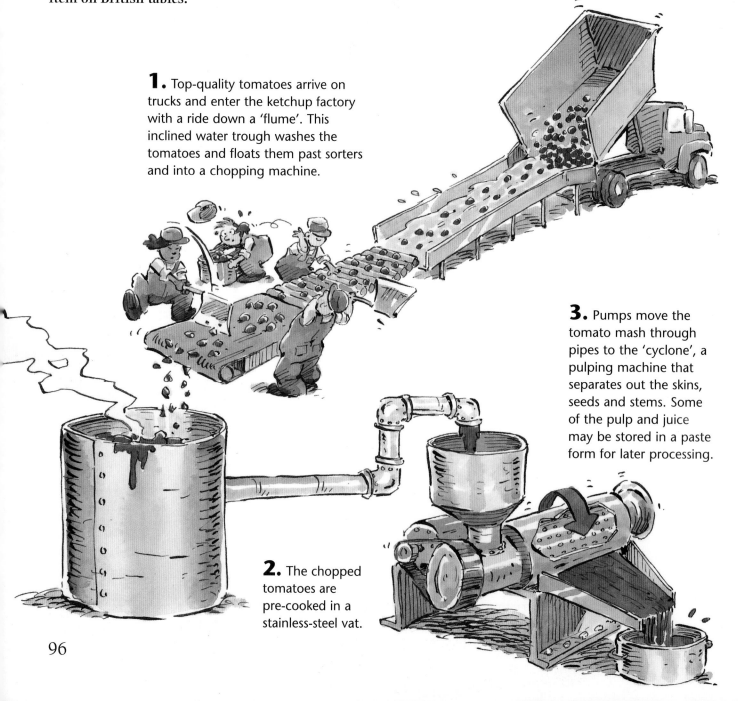

1. Top-quality tomatoes arrive on trucks and enter the ketchup factory with a ride down a 'flume'. This inclined water trough washes the tomatoes and floats them past sorters and into a chopping machine.

3. Pumps move the tomato mash through pipes to the 'cyclone', a pulping machine that separates out the skins, seeds and stems. Some of the pulp and juice may be stored in a paste form for later processing.

2. The chopped tomatoes are pre-cooked in a stainless-steel vat.

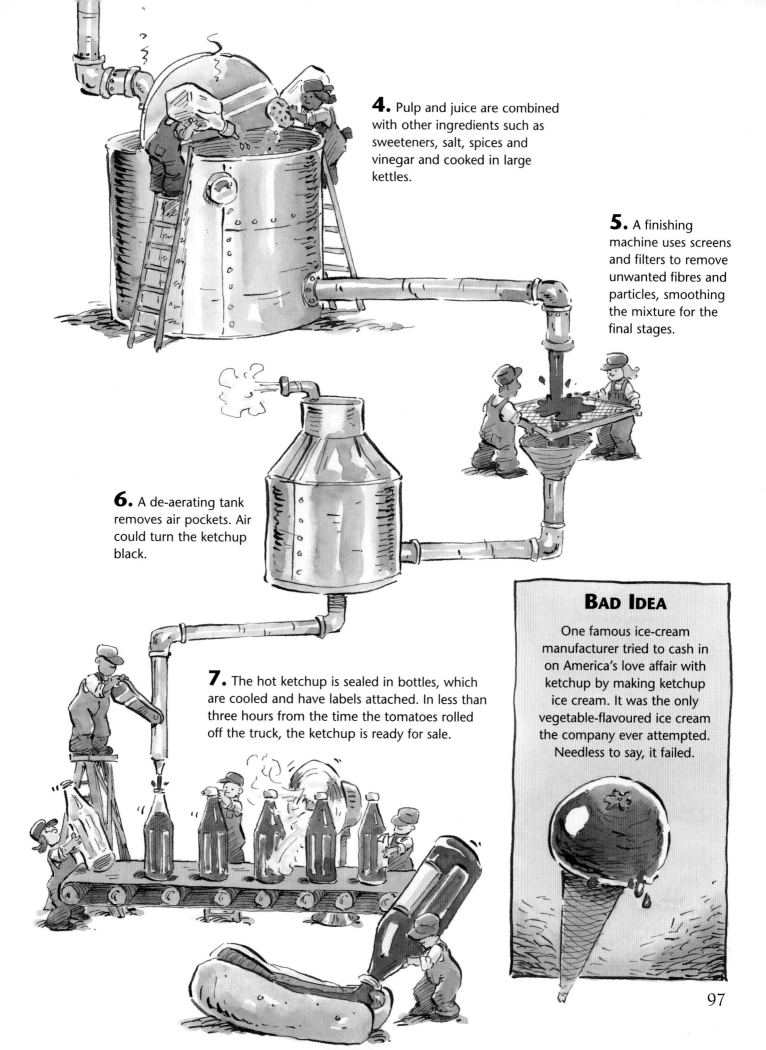

4. Pulp and juice are combined with other ingredients such as sweeteners, salt, spices and vinegar and cooked in large kettles.

5. A finishing machine uses screens and filters to remove unwanted fibres and particles, smoothing the mixture for the final stages.

6. A de-aerating tank removes air pockets. Air could turn the ketchup black.

7. The hot ketchup is sealed in bottles, which are cooled and have labels attached. In less than three hours from the time the tomatoes rolled off the truck, the ketchup is ready for sale.

BAD IDEA

One famous ice-cream manufacturer tried to cash in on America's love affair with ketchup by making ketchup ice cream. It was the only vegetable-flavoured ice cream the company ever attempted. Needless to say, it failed.

Liquorice

When you have a bad cough, what do you reach for? At one time, the answer would have been liquorice – lots of it! People have been chewing on strong-tasting liquorice root for thousands of years to soothe a sore throat. Other than ginseng, liquorice is still the most prescribed herb in China.

And it is one of the oldest sweets in the world. To help make the medicine go down, people later added honey and then sugar to extracts of liquorice root and formed lozenge-shaped cough sweets. Finally, around 1600, Dutch confectioners created liquorice strips – liquorice as we know it today.

1. Dried liquorice roots are ground up and boiled to produce an extract. This extract is dried to a powder and shipped to the sweet factory.

2. The liquorice paste is prepared in big vats, using the company's secret recipe. Liquorice powder, sugar, corn syrup, wheat flour, soya-bean oil, water, preservatives and other ingredients are mixed together to make a slurry.

SWEET ROOT

The liquorice root contains a substance called glycyrrhizin, which is fifty times sweeter than sugar. The extract made from liquorice root is also used to flavour cigars, alcoholic beverages, soft drinks and tobacco.

3. The slurry is pumped into a vertical tube-shaped cooker with revolving blades. An inner pot is enclosed in a metal jacket containing hot steam that cooks the slurry. Some of the water is removed, turning the slurry into a paste.

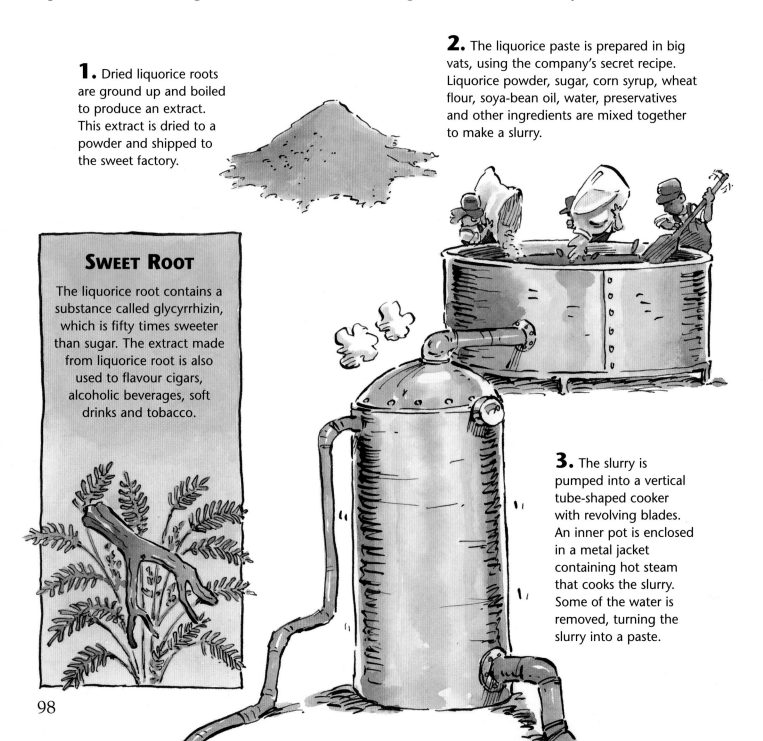

98

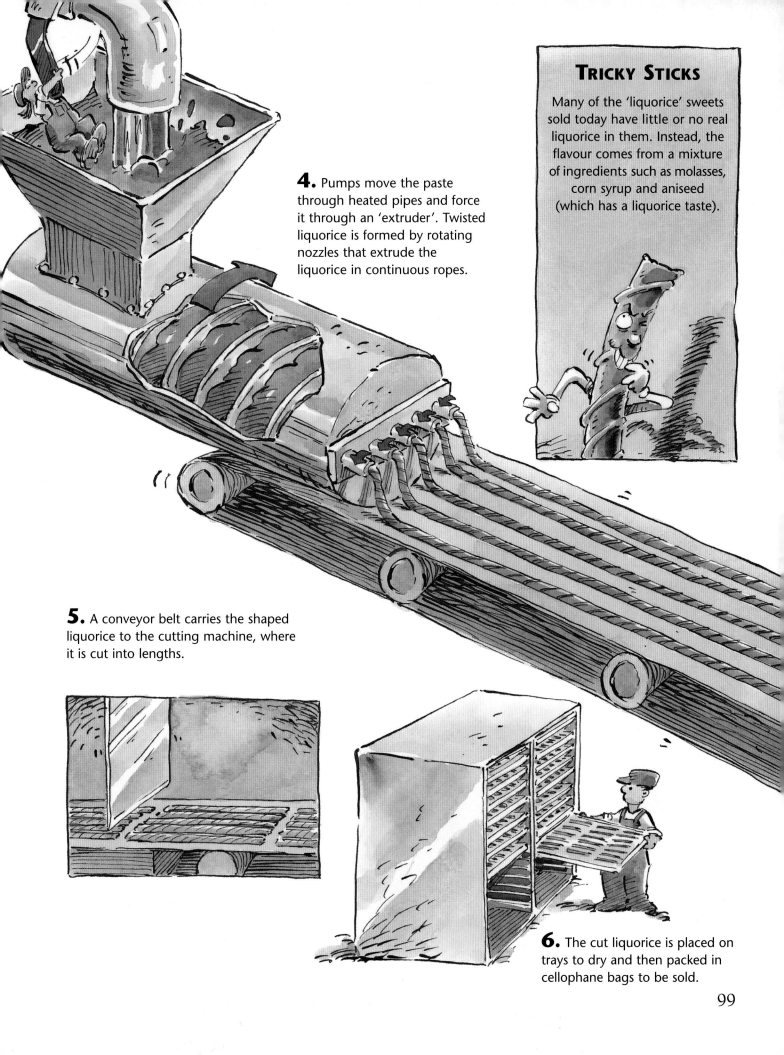

4. Pumps move the paste through heated pipes and force it through an 'extruder'. Twisted liquorice is formed by rotating nozzles that extrude the liquorice in continuous ropes.

TRICKY STICKS

Many of the 'liquorice' sweets sold today have little or no real liquorice in them. Instead, the flavour comes from a mixture of ingredients such as molasses, corn syrup and aniseed (which has a liquorice taste).

5. A conveyor belt carries the shaped liquorice to the cutting machine, where it is cut into lengths.

6. The cut liquorice is placed on trays to dry and then packed in cellophane bags to be sold.

99

Milk

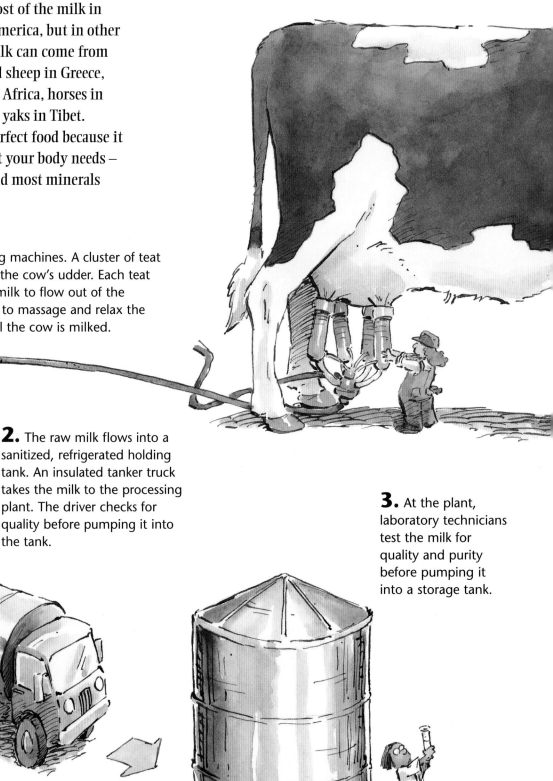

Dairy cows provide most of the milk in Britain and North America, but in other places it's a different story. Milk can come from reindeer in Lapland, goats and sheep in Greece, camels in the deserts of North Africa, horses in Mongolia, llamas in Peru, and yaks in Tibet.

Milk has been called the perfect food because it contains nearly every nutrient your body needs – fat, protein, carbohydrates, and most minerals and vitamins.

1. Most dairy farms use milking machines. A cluster of teat cups is attached to the teats on the cow's udder. Each teat cup applies a vacuum, causing milk to flow out of the udder, and then switches to air, to massage and relax the teat. This rhythm continues until the cow is milked.

2. The raw milk flows into a sanitized, refrigerated holding tank. An insulated tanker truck takes the milk to the processing plant. The driver checks for quality before pumping it into the tank.

3. At the plant, laboratory technicians test the milk for quality and purity before pumping it into a storage tank.

100

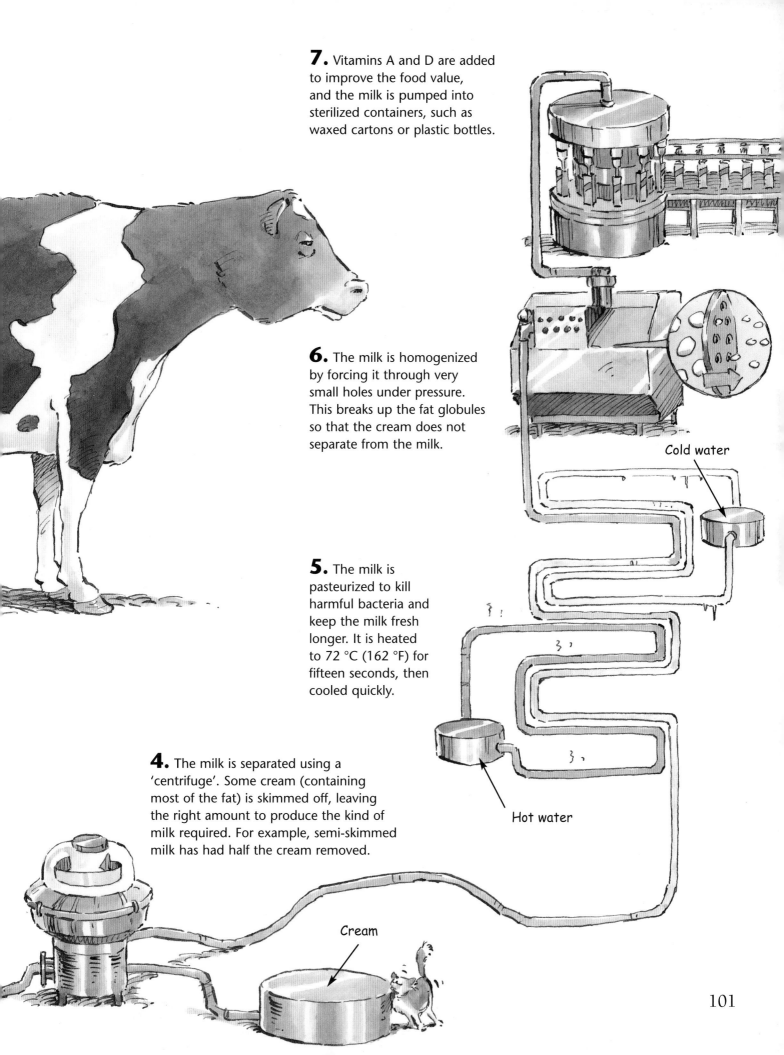

7. Vitamins A and D are added to improve the food value, and the milk is pumped into sterilized containers, such as waxed cartons or plastic bottles.

6. The milk is homogenized by forcing it through very small holes under pressure. This breaks up the fat globules so that the cream does not separate from the milk.

Cold water

5. The milk is pasteurized to kill harmful bacteria and keep the milk fresh longer. It is heated to 72 °C (162 °F) for fifteen seconds, then cooled quickly.

Hot water

4. The milk is separated using a 'centrifuge'. Some cream (containing most of the fat) is skimmed off, leaving the right amount to produce the kind of milk required. For example, semi-skimmed milk has had half the cream removed.

Cream

Pasta

Would you like a plate of little strings for dinner? Or how about some little worms with tomato sauce? If you said 'Yes, please', you probably speak Italian and know the original meaning of the words 'spaghetti' and 'vermicelli'. These are only two of many types of pasta, a nutritious food people have been gobbling up for centuries.

Italians were already enjoying pasta noodles when Marco Polo returned in 1295 to tell stories about Chinese noodles. It is not clear who ate them first.

1. Semolina flour is ground from the heart of a hard variety of wheat known as durum wheat. The flour mill adds B vitamins and dietary iron.

4. The dough is fed into an 'extruder', which forces it through holes the size and shape of the pasta being made. A blade cuts the dough into proper lengths.

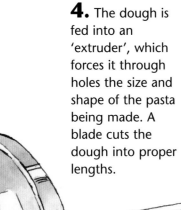

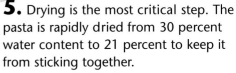

5. Drying is the most critical step. The pasta is rapidly dried from 30 percent water content to 21 percent to keep it from sticking together.

HOLY MACARONI!

Tube-shaped pasta, such as macaroni, has to pass through a die with a centre piece held in place by thin spokes. The fine cuts made by the spokes close up right after extrusion.

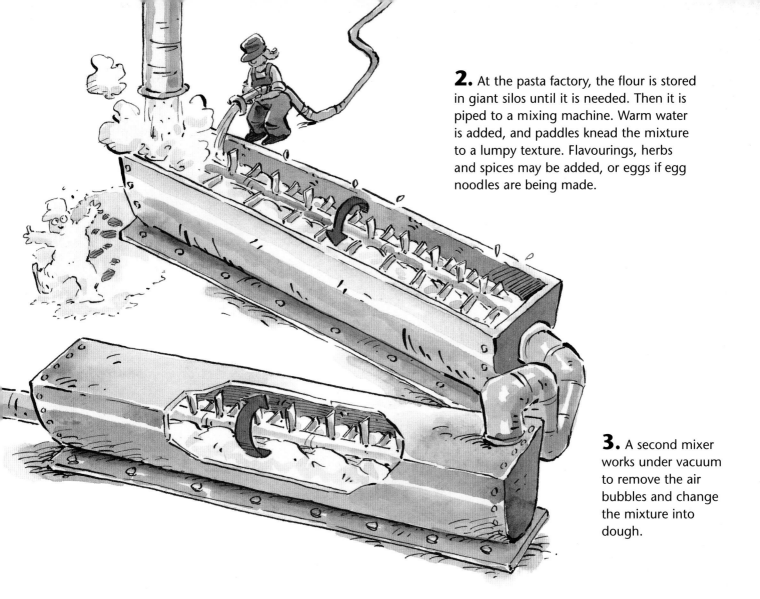

2. At the pasta factory, the flour is stored in giant silos until it is needed. Then it is piped to a mixing machine. Warm water is added, and paddles knead the mixture to a lumpy texture. Flavourings, herbs and spices may be added, or eggs if egg noodles are being made.

3. A second mixer works under vacuum to remove the air bubbles and change the mixture into dough.

6. The pasta now enters the drying tunnel to be slow-dried for thirteen hours, reducing the water content to 12 percent before packaging.

Peanut Butter

Who invented the peanut-butter sandwich? We don't know for sure, but we do know that it was George Washington Carver, an American food-crop researcher, who popularized the peanut as a farm crop. He hoped that peanuts could replace tobacco and cotton, two crops that severely depleted the soil. To prove his point, he invented 300 products that can be made from peanuts, including (*drum roll*) peanut butter!

1. In a special peanut warehouse, blowers, magnets and screens clean the raw peanuts, and conveyor belts carry them to storage silos.

2. From the silo, the peanuts are graded according to size and sent to the shelling machine. Rollers crack the shells, and the peanuts are blown and bounced around until the shells are removed.

3. Another size of grader sorts the peanuts into 'overs' (larger peanuts, which are set aside) and 'troughs' (peanuts of exactly the right size). They are then graded once more for colour and defects and shipped to the peanut-butter factory.

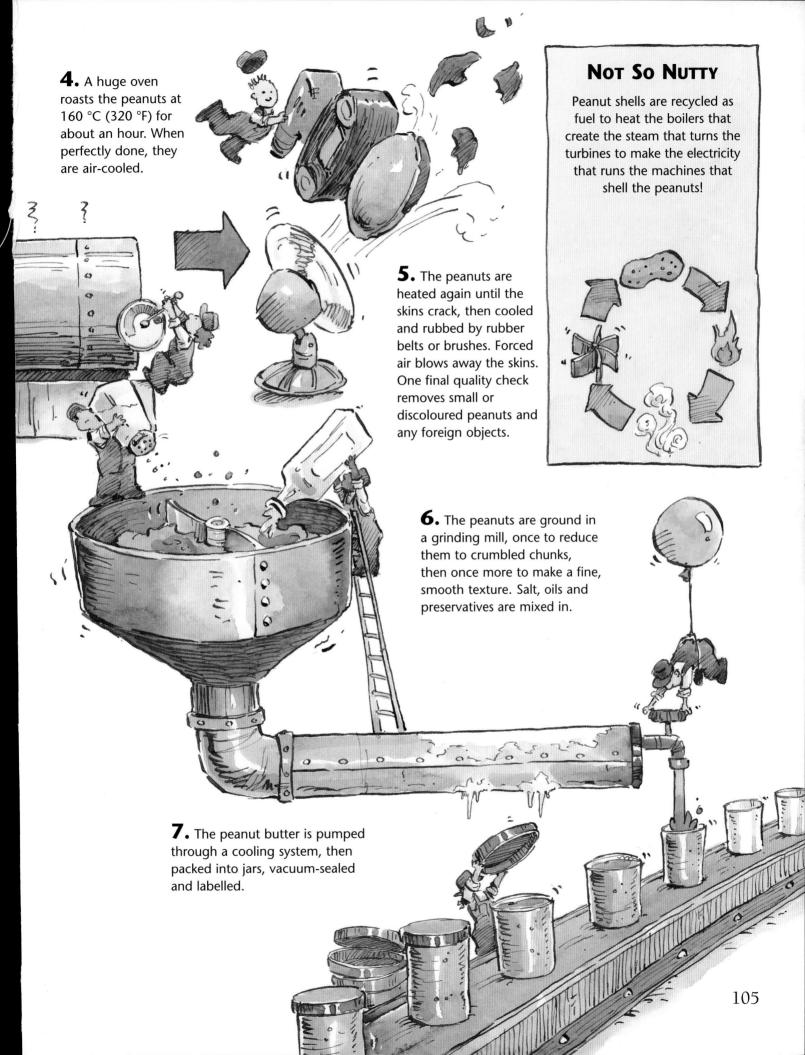

4. A huge oven roasts the peanuts at 160 °C (320 °F) for about an hour. When perfectly done, they are air-cooled.

5. The peanuts are heated again until the skins crack, then cooled and rubbed by rubber belts or brushes. Forced air blows away the skins. One final quality check removes small or discoloured peanuts and any foreign objects.

6. The peanuts are ground in a grinding mill, once to reduce them to crumbled chunks, then once more to make a fine, smooth texture. Salt, oils and preservatives are mixed in.

7. The peanut butter is pumped through a cooling system, then packed into jars, vacuum-sealed and labelled.

NOT SO NUTTY

Peanut shells are recycled as fuel to heat the boilers that create the steam that turns the turbines to make the electricity that runs the machines that shell the peanuts!

Potato Crisps

The story goes that a restaurant customer once complained about French fries that were too thick. The sarcastic chef shaved the potatoes paper thin and sent them back out. People loved them, and another snack food was created.

1. Fresh potatoes are brushed free of dirt and sent down a water trough to the peeler.

2. The peeler removes the skins, which are recycled as animal feed. Cold water rinses away the natural starch, which is sold later to a starch-making plant.

One potato, two potato, three potato, four ...

3. A machine slices the potatoes paper thin. Regular crisps are cut with straight blades and crinkle crisps with ripple blades.

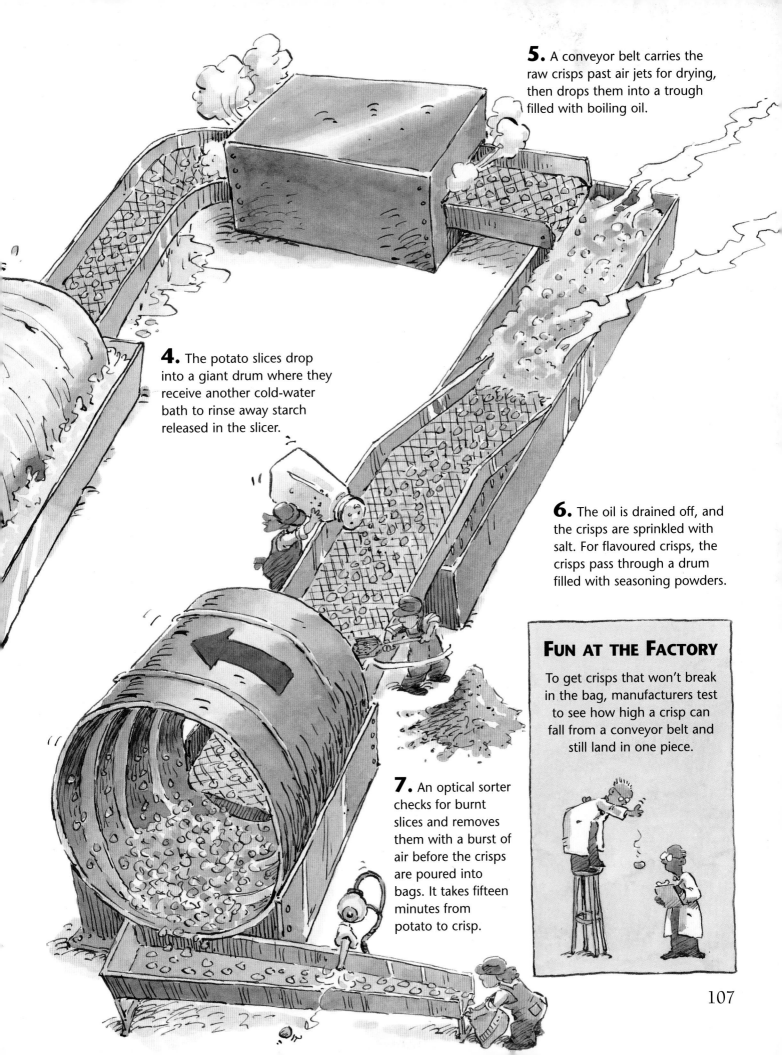

5. A conveyor belt carries the raw crisps past air jets for drying, then drops them into a trough filled with boiling oil.

4. The potato slices drop into a giant drum where they receive another cold-water bath to rinse away starch released in the slicer.

6. The oil is drained off, and the crisps are sprinkled with salt. For flavoured crisps, the crisps pass through a drum filled with seasoning powders.

FUN AT THE FACTORY

To get crisps that won't break in the bag, manufacturers test to see how high a crisp can fall from a conveyor belt and still land in one piece.

7. An optical sorter checks for burnt slices and removes them with a burst of air before the crisps are poured into bags. It takes fifteen minutes from potato to crisp.

107

Salt

In the ancient world, salt was literally worth its weight in gold. The Romans paid their soldiers with precious salt. The word 'salary' in fact comes from the Latin word for salt, *sal*.

Salt is essential for life. The human body needs salt to control the water content of tissues and cells. The earliest humans obtained salt from 'licks' – places where underground salt came to the surface of the Earth. They also got it from the meat of animal prey, which is one reason why hunting became so important.

All salt comes originally from sea water. Even the deposits of rock salt found on every continent come from sea water that evaporated long ago.

2. The salt is hoisted to another grizzly and crusher outside the mine, where it is reduced to pieces about 8 cm (3 in) wide. These are passed under a 'picker', which has magnets to remove unwanted metallic bits.

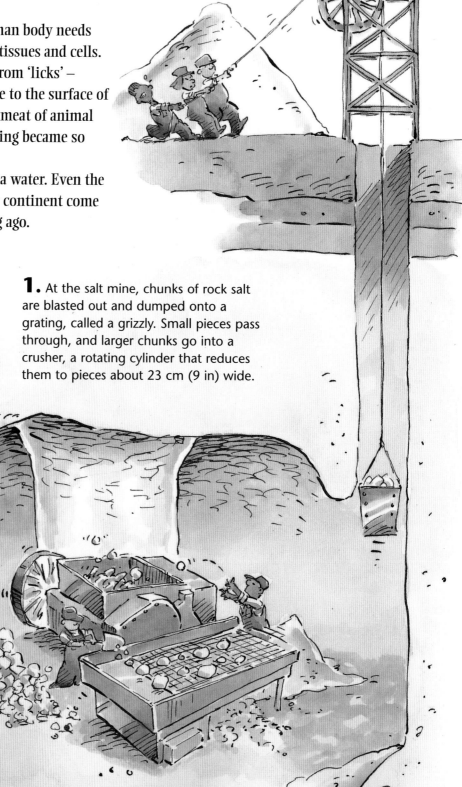

1. At the salt mine, chunks of rock salt are blasted out and dumped onto a grating, called a grizzly. Small pieces pass through, and larger chunks go into a crusher, a rotating cylinder that reduces them to pieces about 23 cm (9 in) wide.

SOLAR SALT

All seas contain salt, but only some inland seas, such as the Great Salt Lake in Utah, USA, contain enough salt to make extraction economical. In this, the oldest of methods, the salty water is pumped through a series of ponds. The Sun evaporates the water, while impurities sink and settle at the bottom of each pond. The salt is washed once more and then piled up to dry.

3. The salt is crushed a third time, yielding pieces about 2.5 cm (1 in) in diameter. These are then ground between rollers, producing a coarse salt that can be used for many purposes, such as softening water or removing ice from roads.

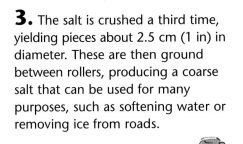

4. To make finer salt, coarse salt is dissolved in water to form brine.

5. The brine is pumped into a 'vacuum evaporator', where it fills the bottoms of a series of three or more cylinders. Steam heat boils the brine in the first cylinder. The steam from this brine heats and boils the brine in the next cylinder, and so on. In the bottom of each cylinder, the salt forms a thick, paste-like slurry.

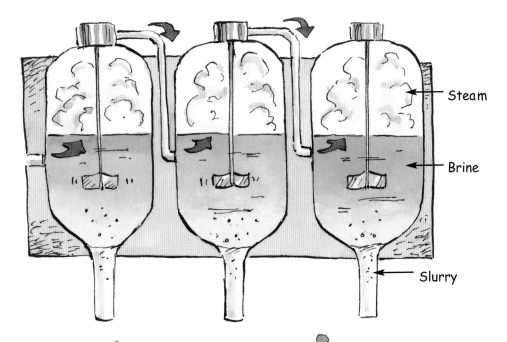

Steam

Brine

Slurry

6. The slurry is filtered, dried, and screened to sort the particles by size. These come out as tiny cubic crystals of salt.

DRILLING FOR SALT

Salt can also be extracted using oil rigs to dig brine wells. Water under high pressure is pumped down one well and passes through a crack in the salt deposit to the other well, dissolving the salt on the way. The brine (salty water) shoots up the second well to the surface, where it is pumped into a vacuum evaporator.

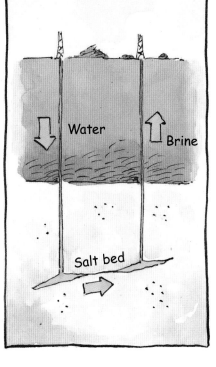

Water

Brine

Salt bed

7. The chemical potassium iodide is added to make iodized table salt. The salt is then bagged and shipped.

109

Tap Water

Earth's sky, land and oceans are filled with water molecules that have moved around on the wind since the beginning of time. Chances are, the water you drink today contains at least one molecule from Cleopatra's bathtub!

Many creatures, such as frogs and whales, live in water. So do invisible creatures, including some deadly bacteria. Some towns and many rural people use water from deep in the Earth. This water is usually safe to drink.

However, most tap water today starts out as surface water in a lake or river. It must be carefully cleaned at water-treatment plants.

1. The water is collected from a lake, river or dammed reservoir on a river system. Because the water has run off the surrounding land, it may contain dirt, dangerous bacteria, metals and chemicals, as well as substances that give it a bad taste, appearance or smell.

3. The water flows to a tank where the chemical chlorine is mixed in to kill bacteria and help break down tiny pieces of organic material (from animals or plants).

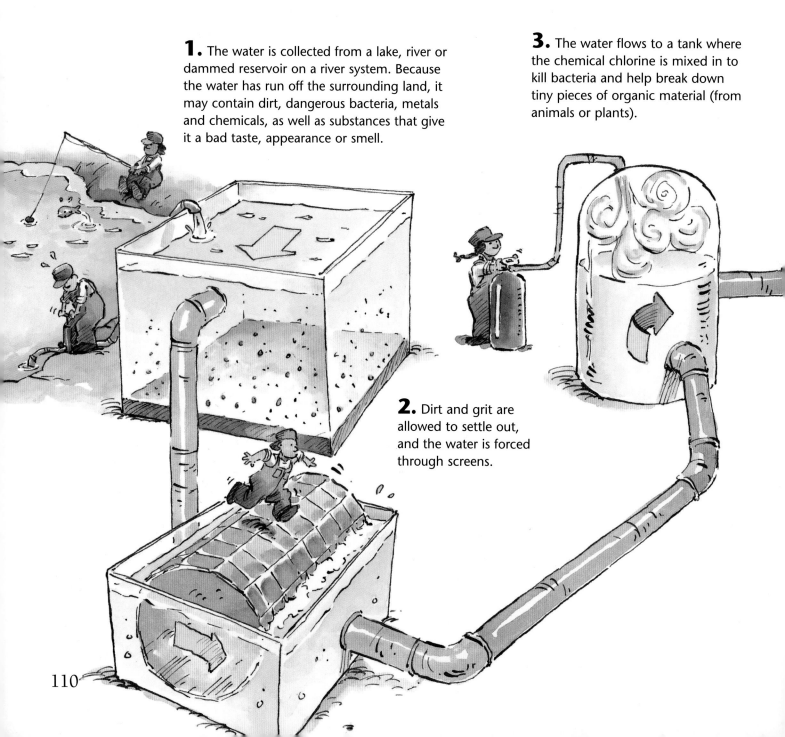

2. Dirt and grit are allowed to settle out, and the water is forced through screens.

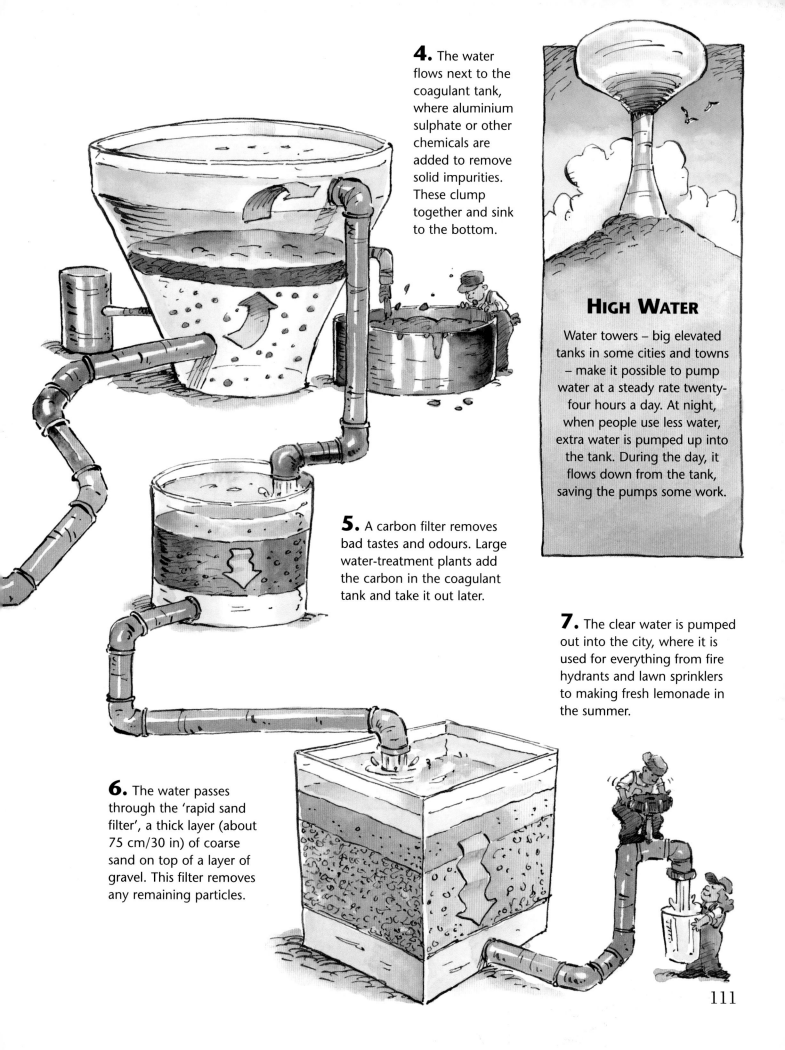

4. The water flows next to the coagulant tank, where aluminium sulphate or other chemicals are added to remove solid impurities. These clump together and sink to the bottom.

HIGH WATER

Water towers – big elevated tanks in some cities and towns – make it possible to pump water at a steady rate twenty-four hours a day. At night, when people use less water, extra water is pumped up into the tank. During the day, it flows down from the tank, saving the pumps some work.

5. A carbon filter removes bad tastes and odours. Large water-treatment plants add the carbon in the coagulant tank and take it out later.

7. The clear water is pumped out into the city, where it is used for everything from fire hydrants and lawn sprinklers to making fresh lemonade in the summer.

6. The water passes through the 'rapid sand filter', a thick layer (about 75 cm/30 in) of coarse sand on top of a layer of gravel. This filter removes any remaining particles.

111

Tea

Tea came to Britain from China in the 1600s. In 1904, a New York merchant named Thomas Sullivan decided to promote his teas by sending out samples stitched into silk bags. His customers discovered that when they soaked the bags in boiling water, they got delicious tea without the mess of loose tea leaves. The teabag was born. Today, tea is the most popular drink in the world.

2. The leaves are twisted and torn into small pieces, releasing their moisture and aroma.

1. Workers handpick the end leaves and buds of the tea bush, which are then dried in the sun for up to twenty hours.

3. To make black tea, the leaves are fermented, then dried with heat. The dried leaves are chopped to the desired fineness. Different-sized screens separate the broken leaves according to size.

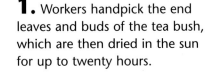

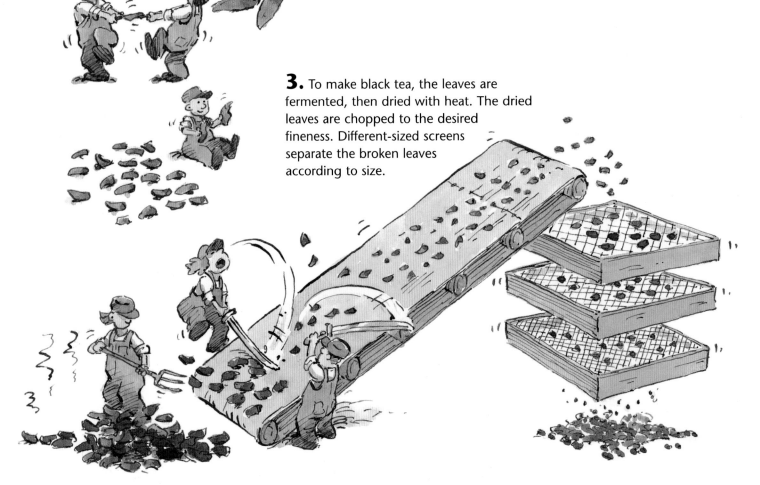

4. The company blend is made using as many as forty types of tea leaves and may include flavourings such as orange peel, peppermint, bergamot and liquorice.

5. For teabags, a machine deposits the tea onto layers of thin paper. Top layers are added to sandwich the tea in place.

6. A heat-sealing drum seals the packets, a perforation blade cuts them into squares, and off they go for packaging.

113

Yogurt

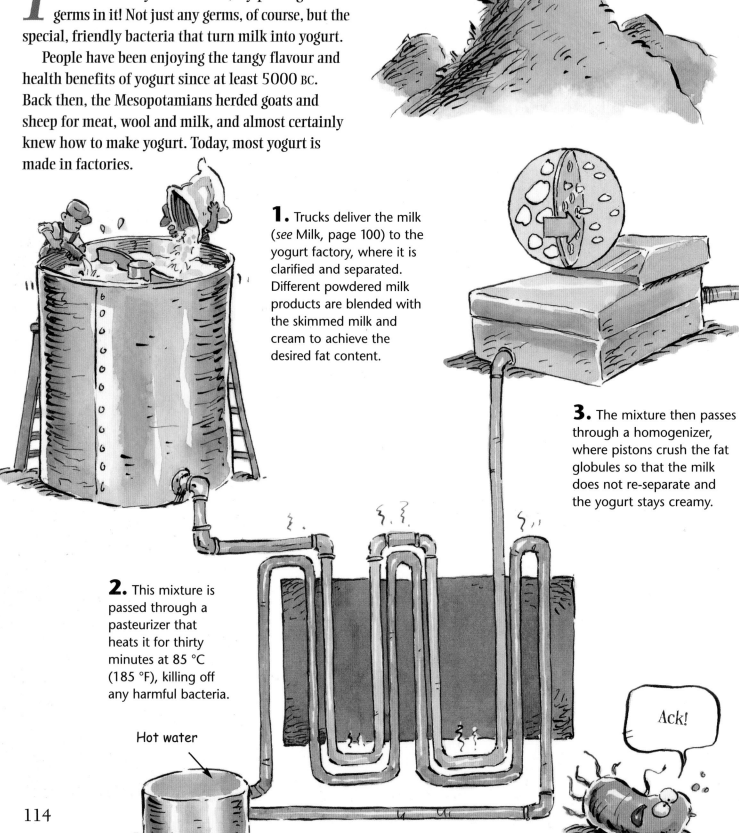

If milk bothers your stomach, try putting some germs in it! Not just any germs, of course, but the special, friendly bacteria that turn milk into yogurt.

People have been enjoying the tangy flavour and health benefits of yogurt since at least 5000 BC. Back then, the Mesopotamians herded goats and sheep for meat, wool and milk, and almost certainly knew how to make yogurt. Today, most yogurt is made in factories.

1. Trucks deliver the milk (*see* Milk, page 100) to the yogurt factory, where it is clarified and separated. Different powdered milk products are blended with the skimmed milk and cream to achieve the desired fat content.

3. The mixture then passes through a homogenizer, where pistons crush the fat globules so that the milk does not re-separate and the yogurt stays creamy.

2. This mixture is passed through a pasteurizer that heats it for thirty minutes at 85 °C (185 °F), killing off any harmful bacteria.

Hot water

Ack!

114

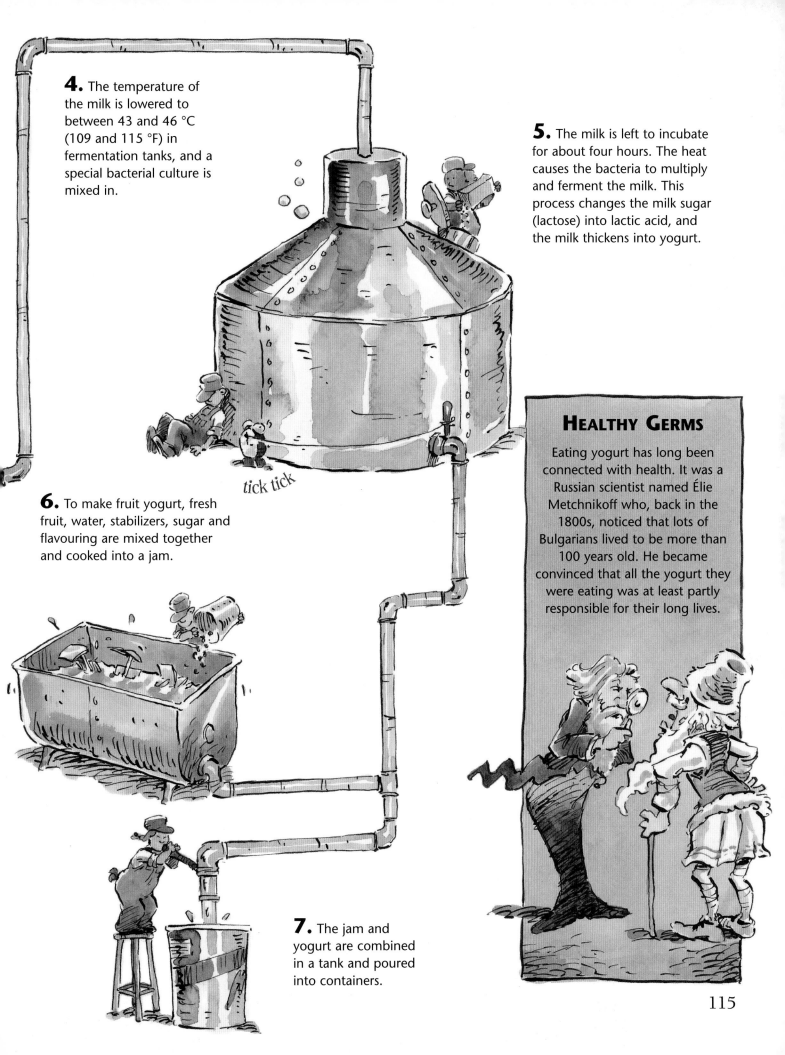

4. The temperature of the milk is lowered to between 43 and 46 °C (109 and 115 °F) in fermentation tanks, and a special bacterial culture is mixed in.

5. The milk is left to incubate for about four hours. The heat causes the bacteria to multiply and ferment the milk. This process changes the milk sugar (lactose) into lactic acid, and the milk thickens into yogurt.

tick tick

6. To make fruit yogurt, fresh fruit, water, stabilizers, sugar and flavouring are mixed together and cooked into a jam.

HEALTHY GERMS

Eating yogurt has long been connected with health. It was a Russian scientist named Élie Metchnikoff who, back in the 1800s, noticed that lots of Bulgarians lived to be more than 100 years old. He became convinced that all the yogurt they were eating was at least partly responsible for their long lives.

7. The jam and yogurt are combined in a tank and poured into containers.

Cover-Ups

Jeans

Jeans were first made for gold miners. In the 1850s, a California dry goods dealer named Levi Strauss stocked work trousers for miners made of strong cotton denim. But true blue jeans were born in 1873, when Strauss teamed up with Jacob Davis, a tailor who had invented a process for reinforcing work trousers with metal rivets. Complaints about damaged desks and saddles later resulted in the removal of the back-pocket rivets. But otherwise, jeans are much the same now as they were 130 years ago.

Denim is woven and dyed in the same factory.

1. Bales of cotton are processed into large spools of yarn (*see* Cotton, page 120), which are run through several vats of indigo-blue dye. The yarn is then dried and coated with sizing (a starchy liquid) to strengthen and stiffen it.

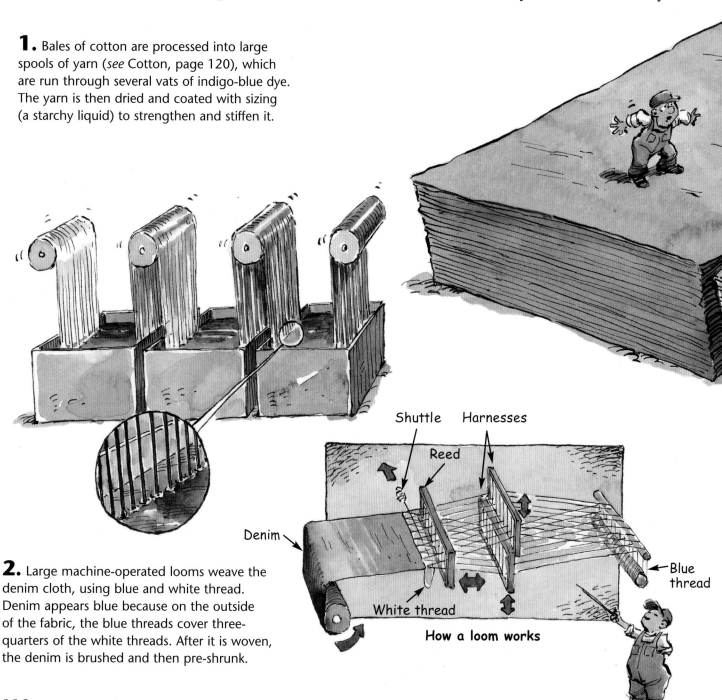

Shuttle   Harnesses

Reed

Denim

White thread

Blue thread

How a loom works

2. Large machine-operated looms weave the denim cloth, using blue and white thread. Denim appears blue because on the outside of the fabric, the blue threads cover three-quarters of the white threads. After it is woven, the denim is brushed and then pre-shrunk.

3. Cutting machines cut out ten to fifteen pattern pieces for each pair of jeans, depending on the design. These machines can cut through a stack 100 layers thick.

REALLY OLD JEANS

Jeans may be named after the sturdy blue trousers worn by sailors in Genoa, Italy, in the 1700s. And the word 'denim' might come from 'serge de Nîmes', an old fabric made in the town of Nîmes, France.

4. In an assembly line, sewing-machine operators sew the parts together. Other workers attach the zips, buttons, rivets and labels, and sew the hems.

119

Cotton

If you wear cotton T-shirts and sleep on cotton sheets, you are one of the millions of people who use cotton fabrics to stay cool in the daytime and warm at night.

Since at least 3000 BC, people in Pakistan and western India have grown the cotton plant to make cloth. Today, it is grown all over the world, especially in warm, sunny regions such as the southern United States and parts of central China.

Cotton plants grow hard seed cases called bolls. At harvest time, the bolls burst open, sprouting long white cotton fibres. In the old days, cotton was picked by hand. It took one person all day to pick the seeds out of a pound of cotton.

Then in 1793, Eli Whitney invented the cotton gin, a machine that could pick the seeds from the fluff fifty times faster. Within ten years, 250 times more cotton was being produced in America than before.

1. Mechanical cotton pickers carefully pull the cotton from the bolls, leaving most of the plant behind.

No Waste

None of the cotton boll is wasted. The bits of cotton left attached to the seeds (called linters) are used to stuff furniture or make rayon (*see* Rayon, page 124). The seeds are crushed to make cooking oil, soap and candles. The rest of the boll is used for animal food or to improve soil.

Dirt and leaves

Seeds

2. The picked cotton is trucked to the 'ginnery'. Cotton gins remove the seeds and other debris from the fibre, and clean and dry it. The fibre is then baled and shipped to the yarn factory.

Bale

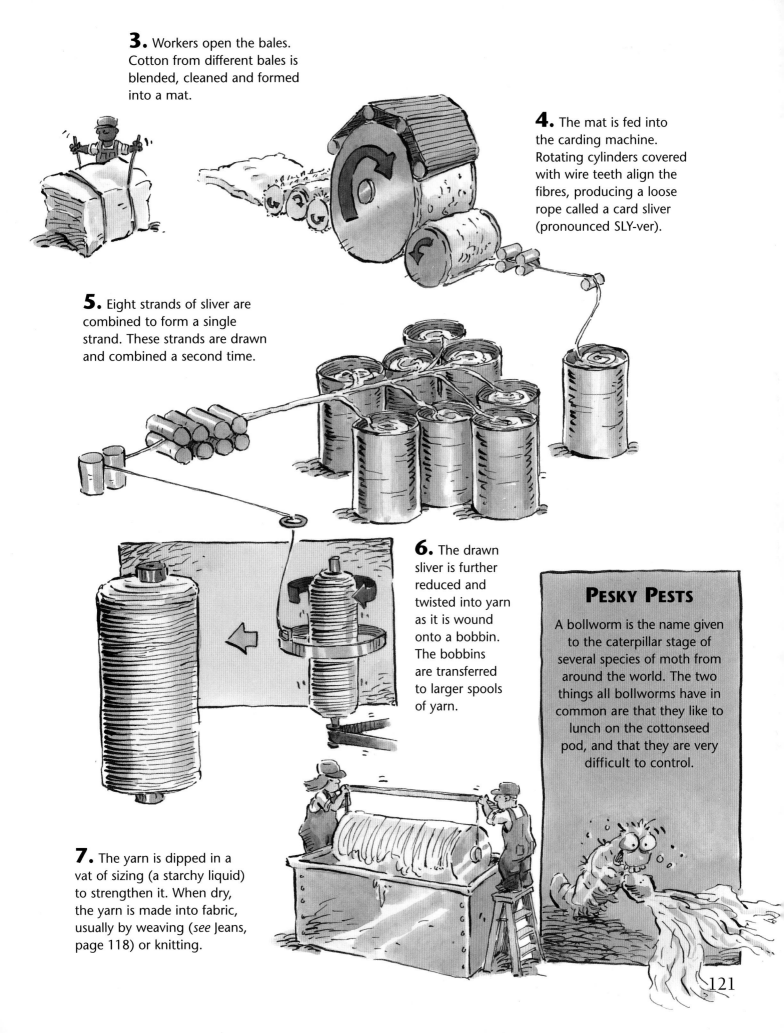

3. Workers open the bales. Cotton from different bales is blended, cleaned and formed into a mat.

4. The mat is fed into the carding machine. Rotating cylinders covered with wire teeth align the fibres, producing a loose rope called a card sliver (pronounced SLY-ver).

5. Eight strands of sliver are combined to form a single strand. These strands are drawn and combined a second time.

6. The drawn sliver is further reduced and twisted into yarn as it is wound onto a bobbin. The bobbins are transferred to larger spools of yarn.

PESKY PESTS

A bollworm is the name given to the caterpillar stage of several species of moth from around the world. The two things all bollworms have in common are that they like to lunch on the cottonseed pod, and that they are very difficult to control.

7. The yarn is dipped in a vat of sizing (a starchy liquid) to strengthen it. When dry, the yarn is made into fabric, usually by weaving (*see* Jeans, page 118) or knitting.

121

Polyester

Have you ever noticed the difference between cotton trousers and polyester trousers when they come out of the dryer? The cotton trousers are all creased, but the polyester trousers are smooth enough to be worn without ironing.

Natural fibres are beautiful, but they tend to crease easily. This was always a big problem – until polyester came along.

The word 'polyester' is made up of two words – 'poly', meaning many, and 'ester', a basic chemical compound. Its main ingredient, ethylene, comes from petroleum (*see* Oil, page 150).

1. Raw polyester is made by combining and heating several chemicals in a vat. The mixture is then extruded (forced out) in a ribbon. When the hot ribbon of polyester cools, it becomes brittle.

STOP THE PRESSES!

Polyester came on the market in 1951, when manufacturers showed off a crease-resistant swimsuit that had been worn for sixty-seven days without being ironed. Soon fabric manufacturers were weaving polyester threads into all their clothing.

2. The ribbon is cut into tiny pieces, which are dried and stored until ready for use.

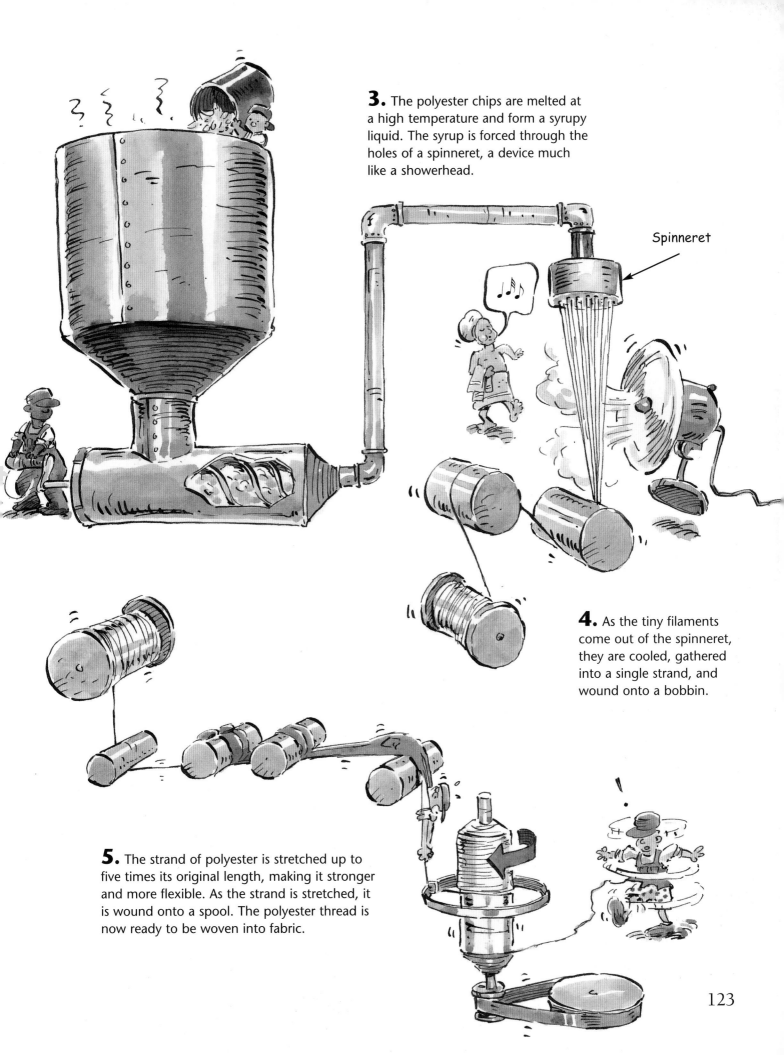

3. The polyester chips are melted at a high temperature and form a syrupy liquid. The syrup is forced through the holes of a spinneret, a device much like a showerhead.

Spinneret

4. As the tiny filaments come out of the spinneret, they are cooled, gathered into a single strand, and wound onto a bobbin.

5. The strand of polyester is stretched up to five times its original length, making it stronger and more flexible. As the strand is stretched, it is wound onto a spool. The polyester thread is now ready to be woven into fabric.

123

Rayon

*D*o you own a rayon shirt, dress or skirt? It feels so soft and silky, you probably wouldn't guess it was made of wood chips!

In fact, rayon was created in France in the 1860s as a substitute for silk. It all happened because some silkworms got sick. Silk manufacturing was an important industry, so the silkworm disease caused a big stir. Luckily, Count Hilaire de Chardonnet came to the rescue with a method of making silk-like fibres from ground-up wood chips and waste from cotton plants.

As it turned out, the silkworms recovered. But the new fabric, rayon, was here to stay.

1. Wood pulp or cotton leftovers are made into pure cellulose (*see* Paper, page 148) and shipped to the rayon factory in big white sheets.

2. The cellulose is soaked in a vat of caustic soda, dried, then put through a shredding machine that turns it into crumbs. The crumbs are aged for up to three days in metal containers.

3. The aged crumbs are churned together with the gas carbon disulphide, which makes the crumbs turn yellow.

4. The 'yellow crumb' is dissolved in a bath of caustic soda, creating a thick, syrupy liquid the colour of honey. The liquid is allowed to age for up to five days and is then filtered to remove impurities.

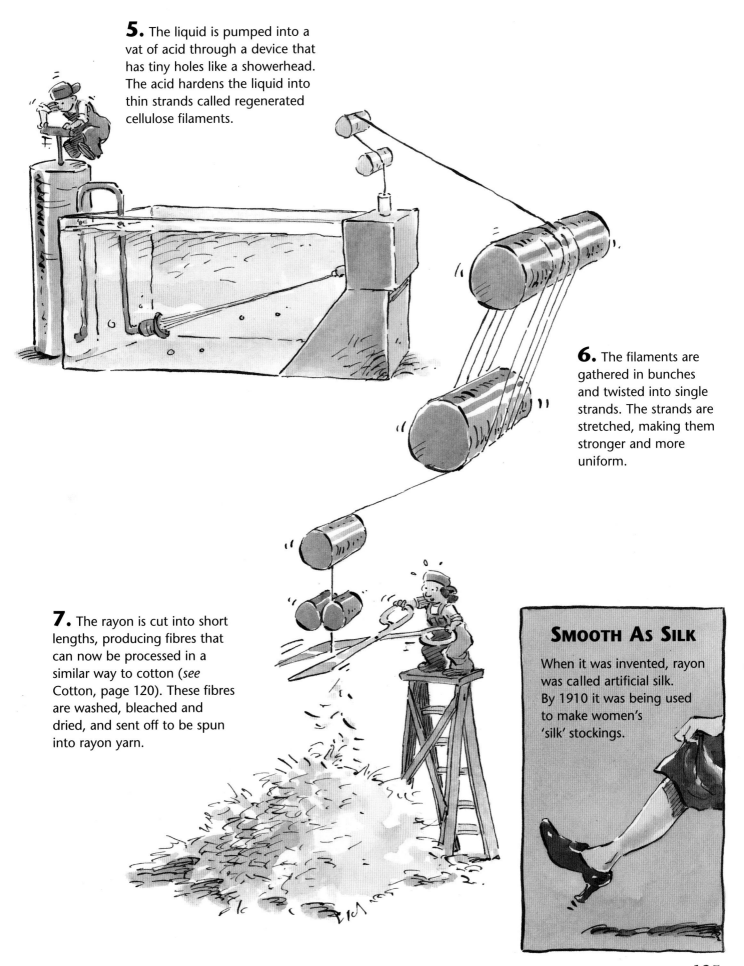

5. The liquid is pumped into a vat of acid through a device that has tiny holes like a showerhead. The acid hardens the liquid into thin strands called regenerated cellulose filaments.

6. The filaments are gathered in bunches and twisted into single strands. The strands are stretched, making them stronger and more uniform.

7. The rayon is cut into short lengths, producing fibres that can now be processed in a similar way to cotton (*see* Cotton, page 120). These fibres are washed, bleached and dried, and sent off to be spun into rayon yarn.

SMOOTH AS SILK

When it was invented, rayon was called artificial silk. By 1910 it was being used to make women's 'silk' stockings.

Trainers

Today, there seem to be more styles of trainers than stars in the sky. To start off, they were just 'running shoes'. It's hard to believe that, until about 100 years ago, people played most sports wearing their everyday shoes – or no shoes at all.

But when the ancient Olympic Games were revived in the late 1800s, competitive sports got a big boost. People wanted shoes specially designed for tennis, football, baseball and running. The first canvas sports shoe was made in the late 1800s, but most people still preferred leather until after World War II, when lighter materials such as nylon took over.

One of the strangest running shoes ever was worn by the Japanese runner who won the Boston Marathon in 1951. Modelled after Japanese shoes, it had the big toe enclosed separately from the rest of the shoe.

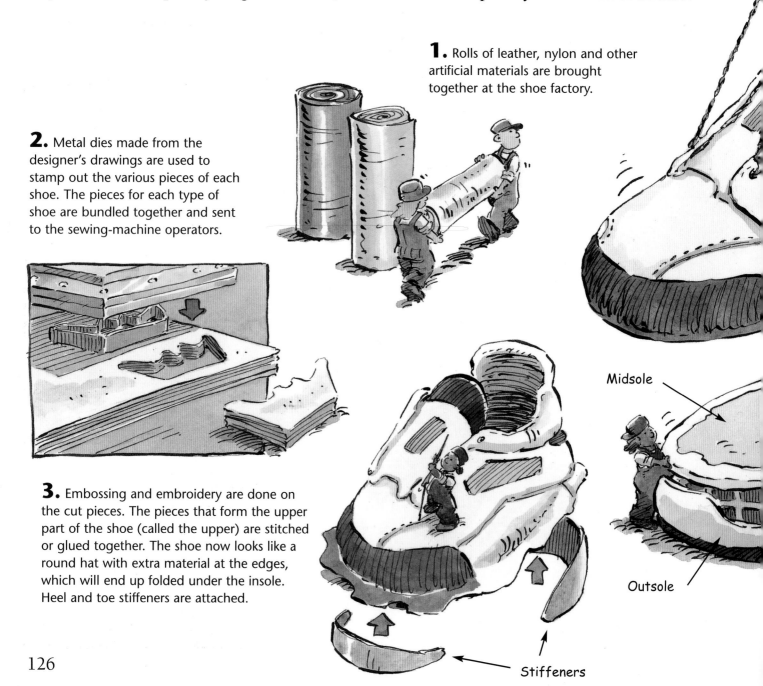

1. Rolls of leather, nylon and other artificial materials are brought together at the shoe factory.

2. Metal dies made from the designer's drawings are used to stamp out the various pieces of each shoe. The pieces for each type of shoe are bundled together and sent to the sewing-machine operators.

3. Embossing and embroidery are done on the cut pieces. The pieces that form the upper part of the shoe (called the upper) are stitched or glued together. The shoe now looks like a round hat with extra material at the edges, which will end up folded under the insole. Heel and toe stiffeners are attached.

Midsole

Outsole

Stiffeners

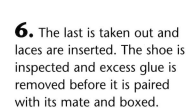

5. The insole is attached to the bottom of a foot-shaped mould called a last. A machine draws the upper snugly over the last, using glue and pressure to attach it to the insole. The midsole/outsole unit is then firmly glued to the upper.

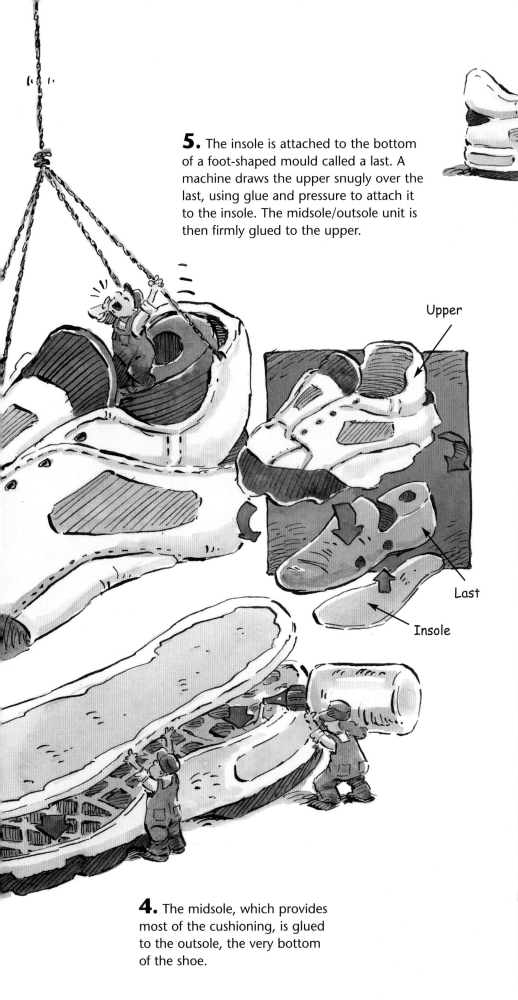

Upper

Last

Insole

4. The midsole, which provides most of the cushioning, is glued to the outsole, the very bottom of the shoe.

6. The last is taken out and laces are inserted. The shoe is inspected and excess glue is removed before it is paired with its mate and boxed.

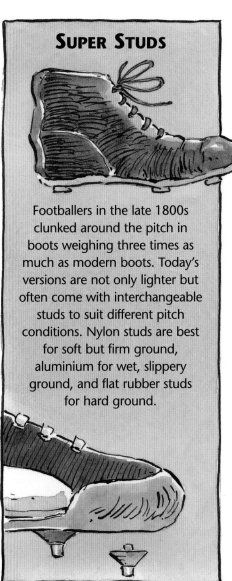

SUPER STUDS

Footballers in the late 1800s clunked around the pitch in boots weighing three times as much as modern boots. Today's versions are not only lighter but often come with interchangeable studs to suit different pitch conditions. Nylon studs are best for soft but firm ground, aluminium for wet, slippery ground, and flat rubber studs for hard ground.

Silk

*T*he story goes that one day long ago, a Chinese princess was relaxing in the palace garden when the cocoon of a silkworm fell from a mulberry tree and landed in her tea. The hot liquid loosened the strands of the cocoon, and the princess discovered silk thread.

That might not be exactly what happened. But modern silk-making, called sericulture, still begins with the silk moth, *Bombyx mori*, which lays a cluster of three or four hundred eggs on a mulberry tree.

1. Silk-makers hatch the best eggs in an incubator and feed the tiny larvae finely chopped mulberry leaves.

2. In twenty to thirty-five days, the larvae grow to about 9 cm (3.5 in) and change colour from grey to pinkish.

Bombyx mori

3. Each larva attaches itself to a rack in the cocoon factory and spins its cocoon, twisting its head back and forth and pushing a double thread out of two glands below its jaws.

4. The thread, called fibroin, is coated with a sticky substance called sericin, which turns hard when exposed to air. The larva, now called a chrysalis, is enclosed completely in the cocoon.

8. The silk thread is removed from the reel and twisted into skeins, which are bundled, baled and shipped off to be made into fabric.

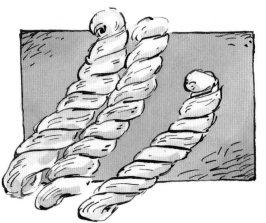

7. Five to eight fibroin threads are fed through a porcelain eyelet and onto a spinning reel. As each cocoon is wound up, the thread of the next is twisted onto the end to create a continuous strand.

6. At the silk factory, the cocoons are sorted for colour and size, then soaked in hot water to soften the sericin and allow the fibroin to separate.

LONG AND STRONG

One cocoon contains as much as 610 m (2000 ft) of silk thread. A thread of silk is stronger than a strand of steel of the same diameter!

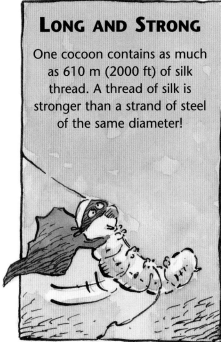

5. Because the strands of fibroin must remain intact to form an unbroken thread, workers use heat to kill the chrysalis before it breaks through.

Wool

Fortunately, we don't have to hunt wild animals to give us warm clothing anymore. By 4000 BC, people in Sumeria (now Iraq) had learned how to weave natural materials into fabric. Sheep's wool was the warmest, so herds of sheep were raised for their wool, as well as for milk and meat.

Wool sweaters start out in the springtime, when the sheep are ready for shearing.

1. The sheep is held down, and its feet are tied together. The shearer removes the wool with electric shears, then releases the sheep to run off and start growing another coat. The sheared wool is called a fleece.

2. The fleece of each sheep is kept together so a grader can separate the best-quality wool (the wool from the shoulders and sides) from the rest.

3. The raw wool is put into a scouring tub, which washes away the dirt, grease and dried sheep sweat. Rollers squeeze out most of the water.

4. The wool fibres go into a carding machine – a series of rollers with brush-like metal teeth – which straightens and further cleans the fibres, forming it into long bands called slivers.

Slivers

Roving

5. The slivers are further compacted, drawn out, and twisted to form pencil-thick strands called roving. The roving is then spun into yarn and wound onto bobbins.

6. The bobbins of yarn are put into large vats of dye.

Yarn

7. When the yarn has dried, it is ready to be shipped off to be woven into fabric or knitted into clothing.

RABBIT WOOL?

Besides sheep, certain kinds of camels, goats and rabbits grow hair that is called wool.

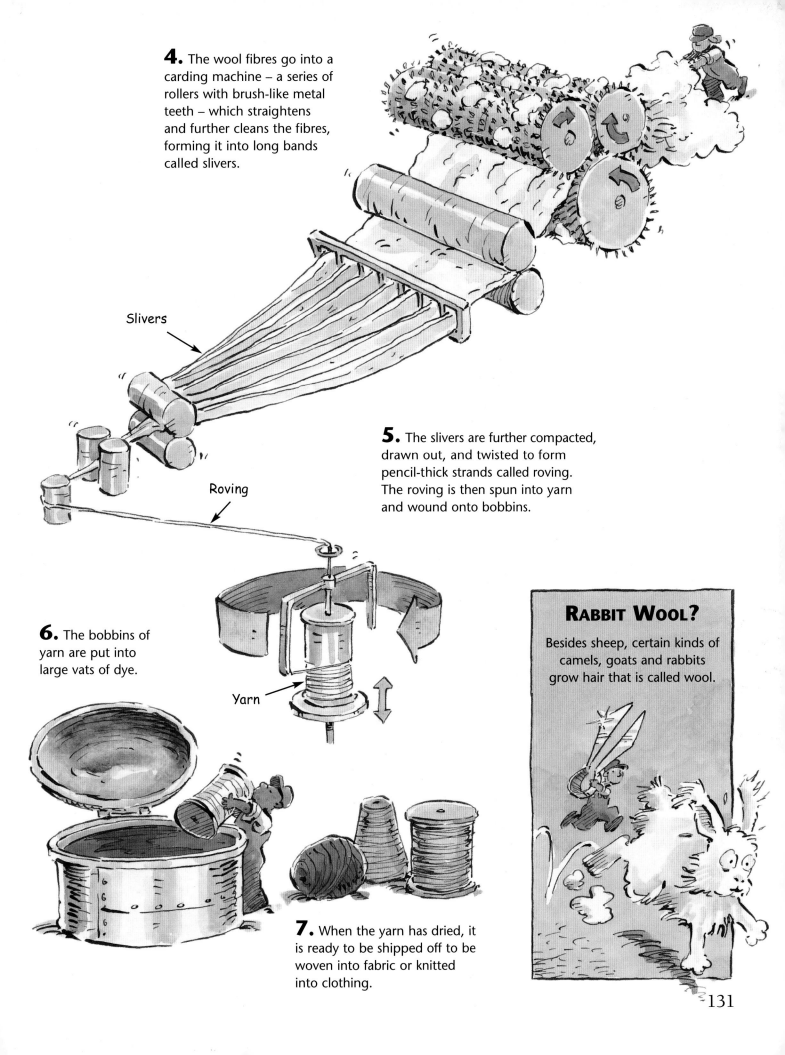

131

Work Gloves

People have been wearing coverings on their hands since the beginning of time, protecting themselves from the cold, heat and nasty pointed bits that nature throws at them. Modern work gloves are made out of all kinds of materials, from leather to latex. PVC gloves are coated in polyvinyl chloride, a type of plastic closely related to polythene (*see* Plastic Resins, page 152). PVC is used in everything from water pipes to raincoats. Gloves made from this material are durable, waterproof and chemical-proof, and are worn by workers in a whole range of industries, such as fishing and oil.

1. Using a metal die, a hydraulic press stamps out the cotton flannel pieces that make up the glove. Up to twenty pieces can be cut at a time.

2. A sewing machine operator sews the pieces together inside out. An elastic cuff is sewn on last.

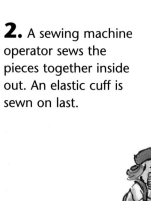

4. To make PVC gloves, an inside liner is made as described in the first three steps. These are slipped onto metal hand-shaped forms that have detachable thumbs for easy removal at the end of the process.

3. A machine turns the gloves right side out and heat-presses them on hand-shaped moulds. They are dropped onto a conveyor, inspected and paired.

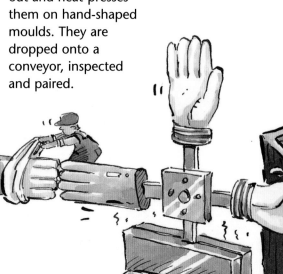

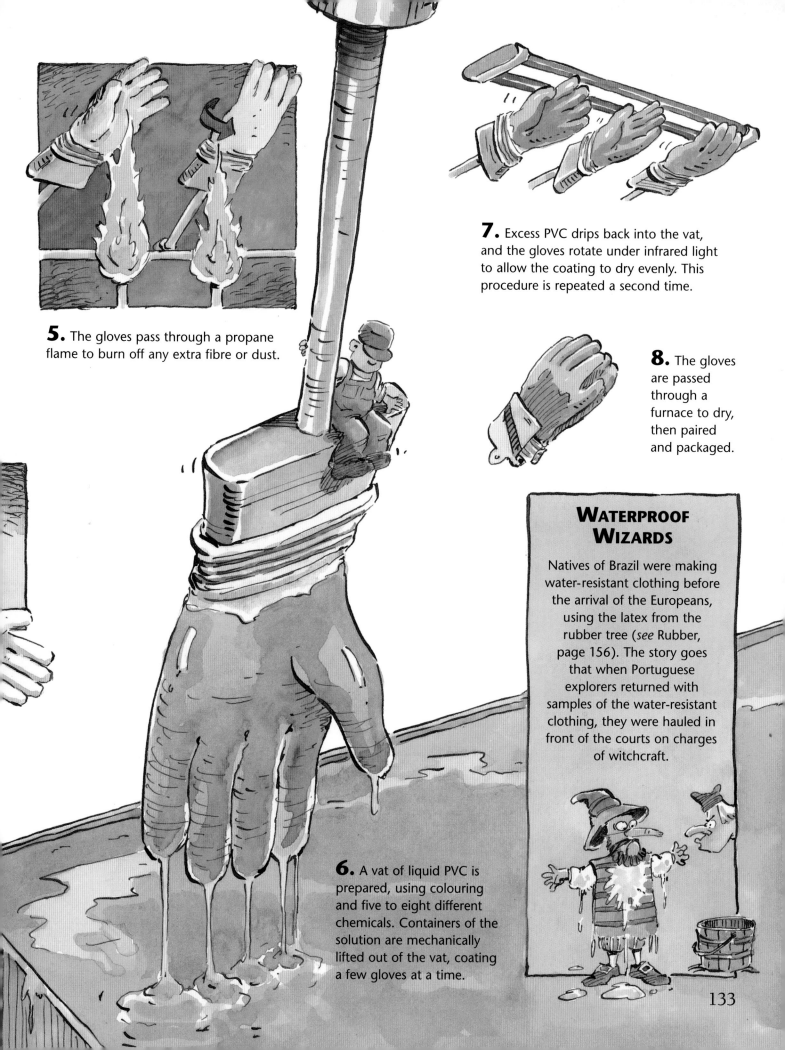

5. The gloves pass through a propane flame to burn off any extra fibre or dust.

6. A vat of liquid PVC is prepared, using colouring and five to eight different chemicals. Containers of the solution are mechanically lifted out of the vat, coating a few gloves at a time.

7. Excess PVC drips back into the vat, and the gloves rotate under infrared light to allow the coating to dry evenly. This procedure is repeated a second time.

8. The gloves are passed through a furnace to dry, then paired and packaged.

WATERPROOF WIZARDS

Natives of Brazil were making water-resistant clothing before the arrival of the Europeans, using the latex from the rubber tree (*see* Rubber, page 156). The story goes that when Portuguese explorers returned with samples of the water-resistant clothing, they were hauled in front of the courts on charges of witchcraft.

133

Back to Basics

Aluminium

Aluminium is the Earth's most abundant metal, but it never appears in its pure form. It likes to combine with other elements and water to form an ore called bauxite.

Most bauxite is found in tropical and subtropical countries, such as Jamaica, and it's easy to dig up. The complicated part is getting the bauxite to give up its aluminium. For one thing, it takes a lot of electricity, and that means shipping the bauxite to developed countries that have large supplies of electricity at a reasonable cost.

So let's start with 5 tonnes of bauxite and see what happens.

1. The bauxite rocks are crushed into a powder.

2. The powder is mixed with caustic soda (lime and soda ash) and water and passed into a 'digester', where it softens into a paste. Under pressure and heat, the caustic soda combines with the alumina (the stuff they're trying to separate out) to form a new material called sodium aluminate.

SAVE YOUR ENERGY

It pays to recycle aluminium cans. The energy needed to produce recycled aluminium is less than 5 percent of that needed to make the original metal.

3. The unneeded part of the ore (known as red mud) is filtered out and pumped away.

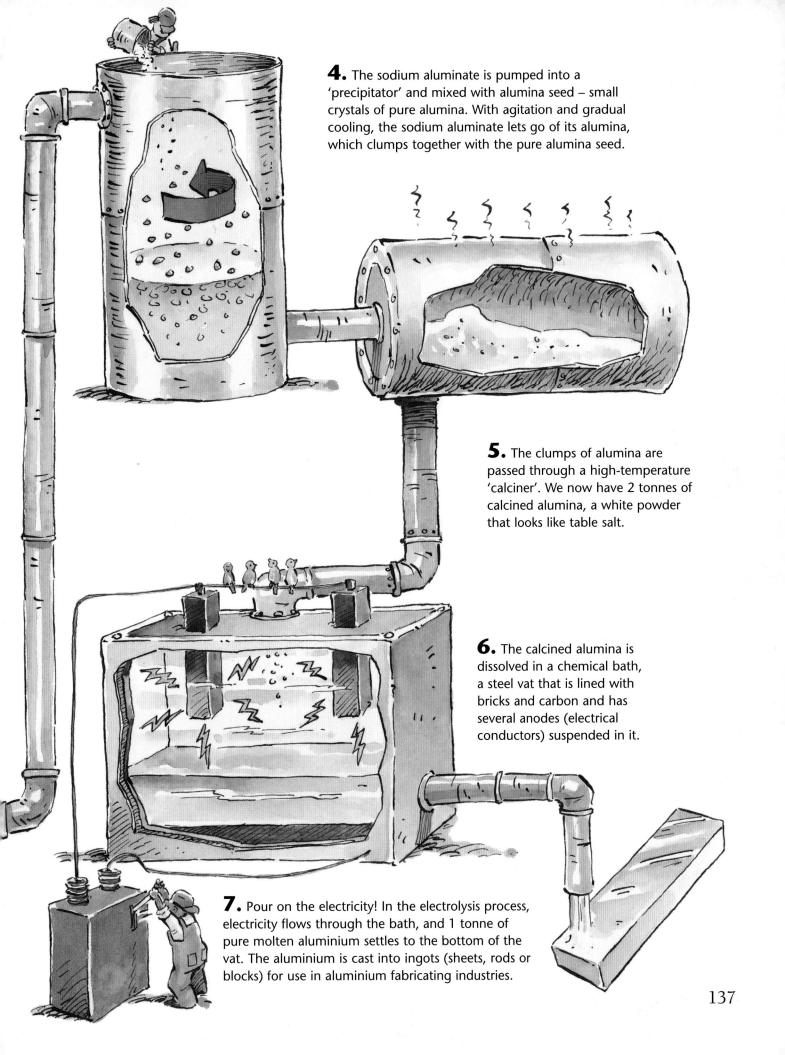

4. The sodium aluminate is pumped into a 'precipitator' and mixed with alumina seed – small crystals of pure alumina. With agitation and gradual cooling, the sodium aluminate lets go of its alumina, which clumps together with the pure alumina seed.

5. The clumps of alumina are passed through a high-temperature 'calciner'. We now have 2 tonnes of calcined alumina, a white powder that looks like table salt.

6. The calcined alumina is dissolved in a chemical bath, a steel vat that is lined with bricks and carbon and has several anodes (electrical conductors) suspended in it.

7. Pour on the electricity! In the electrolysis process, electricity flows through the bath, and 1 tonne of pure molten aluminium settles to the bottom of the vat. The aluminium is cast into ingots (sheets, rods or blocks) for use in aluminium fabricating industries.

137

Brick

Remember the Three Little Pigs? The Big Bad Wolf flattened the straw and wooden houses with just a huff and a puff. But the brick house ...

Brick was first fired (baked) in the Middle East around 4000 BC. When fired at a high temperature, bricks were very strong, and making them was a lot easier than carving blocks out of natural stone. After the fall of the Roman Empire, brick-making almost died out. The Dutch brought it back into use in Europe in the 1200s.

By the 1900s, a great many buildings and even roads were made of brick. Today, brick is just one of many building materials. To compete, manufacturers have developed faster methods and lighter bricks. But you still can't blow 'em down!

1. Natural materials such as kaolin (a fine white clay) and shale are crushed and ground. A screen separates out the correct size of particles.

2. The ground particles and water are mixed by rotating knives in a 'pug mill', and the mixture is sent to an extruder.

3. The extruder forces the mixture through a die (a metal piece that shapes the brick), creating a continuous length called a slug.

4. The fired shale will produce red-coloured bricks. If another colour is desired, the slug is coated with sand containing different minerals (such as zinc or iron).

138

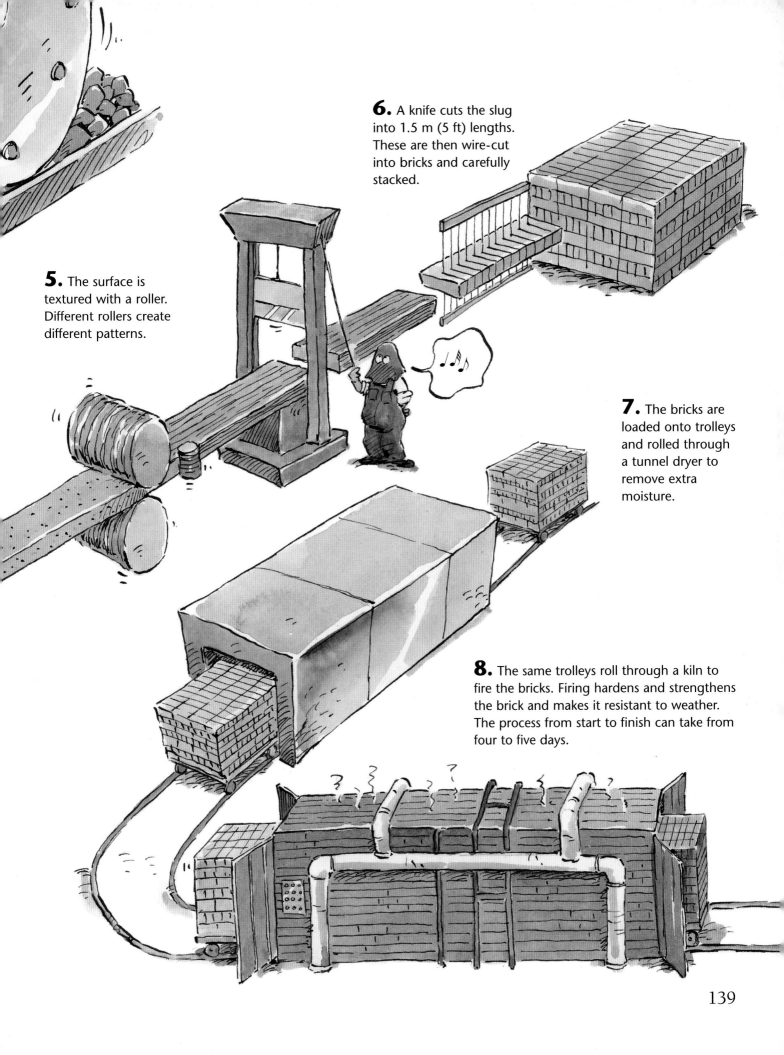

6. A knife cuts the slug into 1.5 m (5 ft) lengths. These are then wire-cut into bricks and carefully stacked.

5. The surface is textured with a roller. Different rollers create different patterns.

7. The bricks are loaded onto trolleys and rolled through a tunnel dryer to remove extra moisture.

8. The same trolleys roll through a kiln to fire the bricks. Firing hardens and strengthens the brick and makes it resistant to weather. The process from start to finish can take from four to five days.

Cement

*I*n the movies, the bad guys sometimes fit their enemies with cement shoes. These are not meant for dancing!

In the real world, you're more likely to see cement in a pavement. Cement is the name for any material that can be used to stick things together. But most often, cement means hydraulic cement, which starts out as a powder until you add water, and then it hardens. This hardening is a chemical reaction, not just a matter of drying out. And once cement hardens, water will not make it soft.

The Romans, who mixed volcanic ash and burnt limestone, made the best cement in the ancient world. Then people forgot how to make cement until 1756, when John Smeaton reinvented it while building the Eddystone lighthouse near Plymouth, England. Today, hundreds of millions of tonnes of cement are made and used in the world every year.

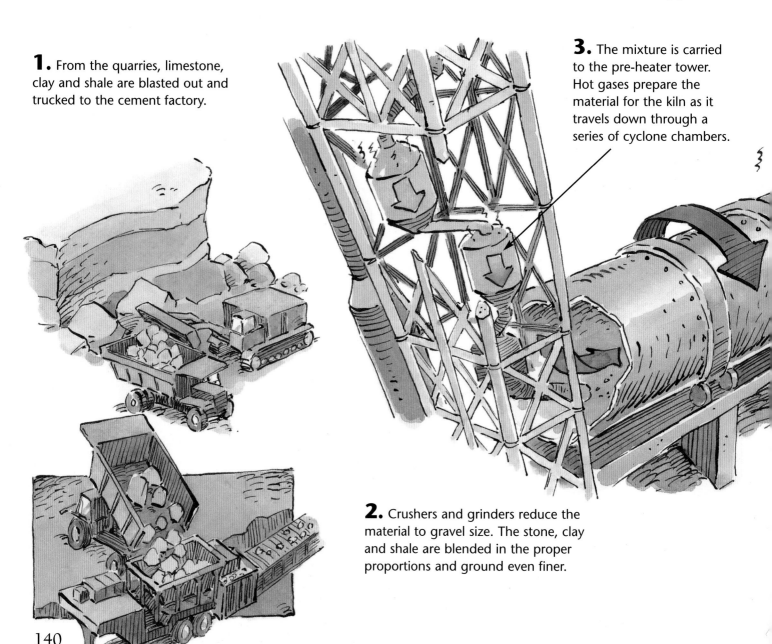

1. From the quarries, limestone, clay and shale are blasted out and trucked to the cement factory.

3. The mixture is carried to the pre-heater tower. Hot gases prepare the material for the kiln as it travels down through a series of cyclone chambers.

2. Crushers and grinders reduce the material to gravel size. The stone, clay and shale are blended in the proper proportions and ground even finer.

7. When ready for shipping, the cement is either bagged or shipped by truck or rail to concrete producers.

6. The clinkers are cooled and sent to a ball mill (a rotating steel drum filled with steel balls) and ground fine. Gypsum is added, and the finished cement is stored.

Clinkers

4. The raw mix tumbles through the kiln, a huge rotating cylinder that is set on a downward angle and is heated by flames that reach 1870 °C (3400 °F).

5. The intense heat causes the chemical reaction necessary to create cement. The material comes out of the kiln transformed into red-hot pebbles called clinkers.

CONCRETE EXAMPLES

Portland cement got its name from stone quarried on England's Isle of Portland. In 1824, Joseph Aspdin noticed that his limestone-and-clay mixture, when set, looked just like Portland stone.

When Portland cement is mixed with sand, water and small stones, crystals form and bind the materials together into concrete. This rock-hard material is used for roads, pavements, buildings and all kinds of other structures – even tables and countertops.

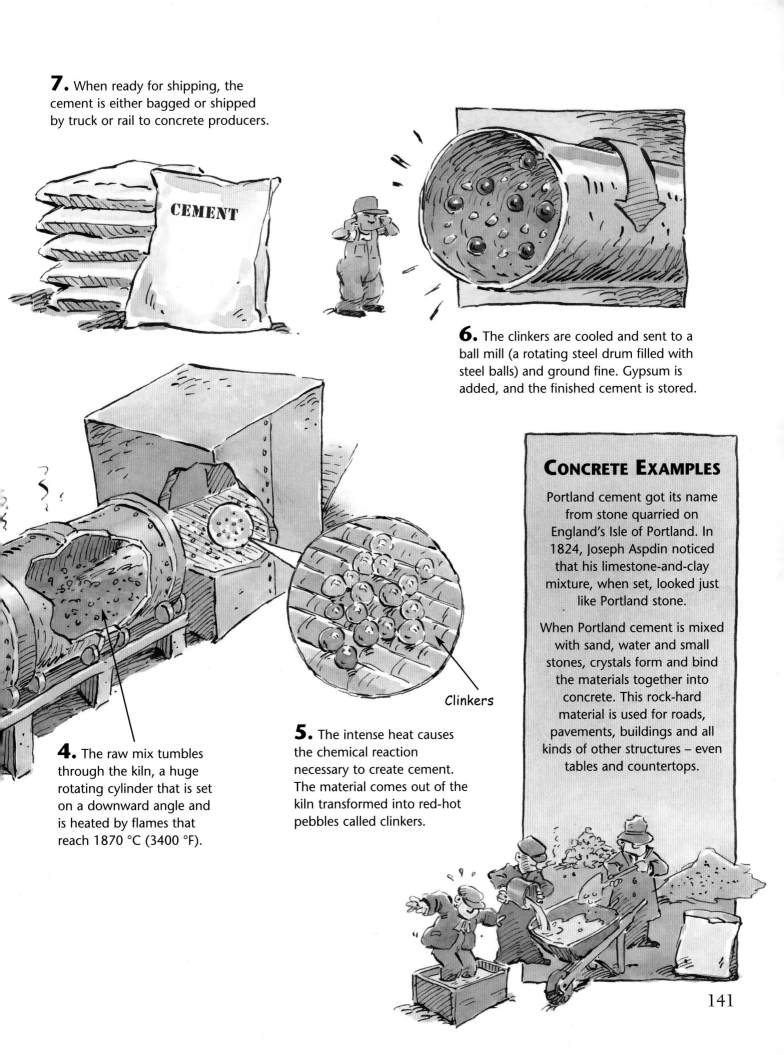

Glass

When you think of glass, you probably think of windows, bottles and mirrors – glass that shatters when hit by a rock. But what about bulletproof glass, fibreglass, and glass used for building blocks? Glass ceramics appear on the nose cones of guided missiles. And glass optical fibres carry information at incredible speeds to computers around the world.

Glass is basically sand (silica) with a little limestone, soda and a few other things mixed in. It can be shaped in many ways, including blowing, pressing, drawing and casting, depending on what it will be used for. This is how most flat glass is made, in a continuous process that runs day and night.

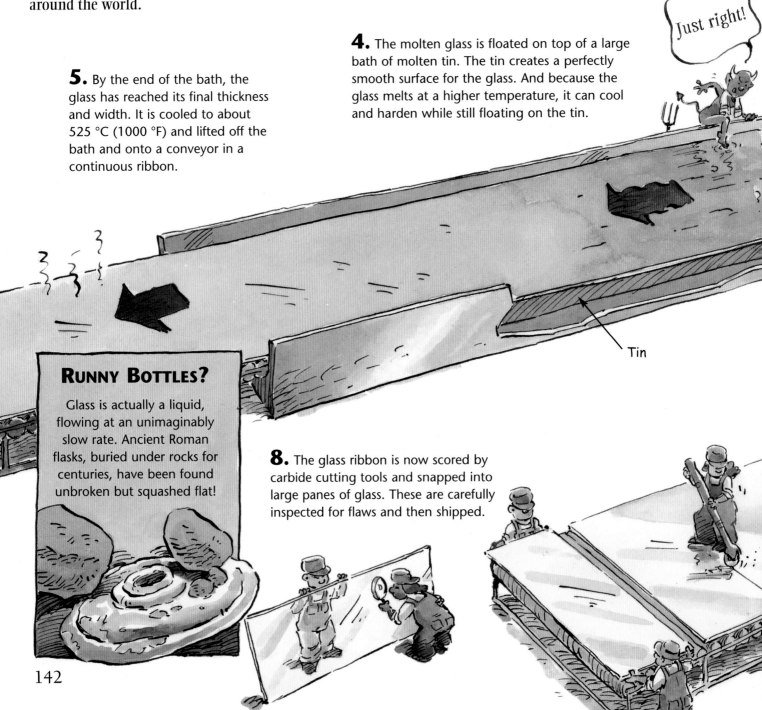

4. The molten glass is floated on top of a large bath of molten tin. The tin creates a perfectly smooth surface for the glass. And because the glass melts at a higher temperature, it can cool and harden while still floating on the tin.

Just right!

5. By the end of the bath, the glass has reached its final thickness and width. It is cooled to about 525 °C (1000 °F) and lifted off the bath and onto a conveyor in a continuous ribbon.

Tin

RUNNY BOTTLES?

Glass is actually a liquid, flowing at an unimaginably slow rate. Ancient Roman flasks, buried under rocks for centuries, have been found unbroken but squashed flat!

8. The glass ribbon is now scored by carbide cutting tools and snapped into large panes of glass. These are carefully inspected for flaws and then shipped.

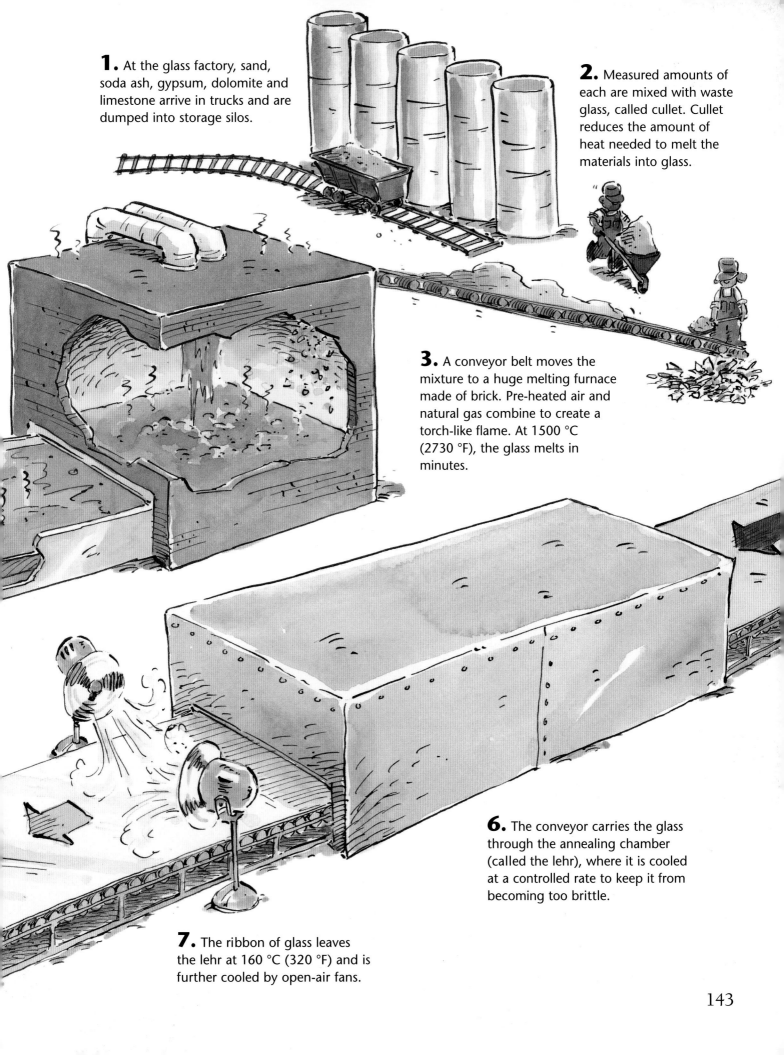

1. At the glass factory, sand, soda ash, gypsum, dolomite and limestone arrive in trucks and are dumped into storage silos.

2. Measured amounts of each are mixed with waste glass, called cullet. Cullet reduces the amount of heat needed to melt the materials into glass.

3. A conveyor belt moves the mixture to a huge melting furnace made of brick. Pre-heated air and natural gas combine to create a torch-like flame. At 1500 °C (2730 °F), the glass melts in minutes.

6. The conveyor carries the glass through the annealing chamber (called the lehr), where it is cooled at a controlled rate to keep it from becoming too brittle.

7. The ribbon of glass leaves the lehr at 160 °C (320 °F) and is further cooled by open-air fans.

143

Iron and Steel

*I*t's nice when something you need falls from the sky. That's actually what happened about 6000 years ago when people discovered pure iron in meteorites. This hard substance was fine for making tools and weapons. But it wasn't until about 1000 BC that most people in the world had figured out how to separate iron from other rocks and use it to make more complicated things such as armour.

But iron broke easily, so people kept looking for stronger metals. Eventually, some Iron Age people found ways to make alloys (chemical mixtures) of iron and other substances. That was the beginning, but far from the end, of steel. Better alloys and methods were invented and continue to be developed today.

Most steel now is made using the basic oxygen process. The process of transforming iron to steel mainly consists of removing impurities such as carbon and alloying other materials with the iron.

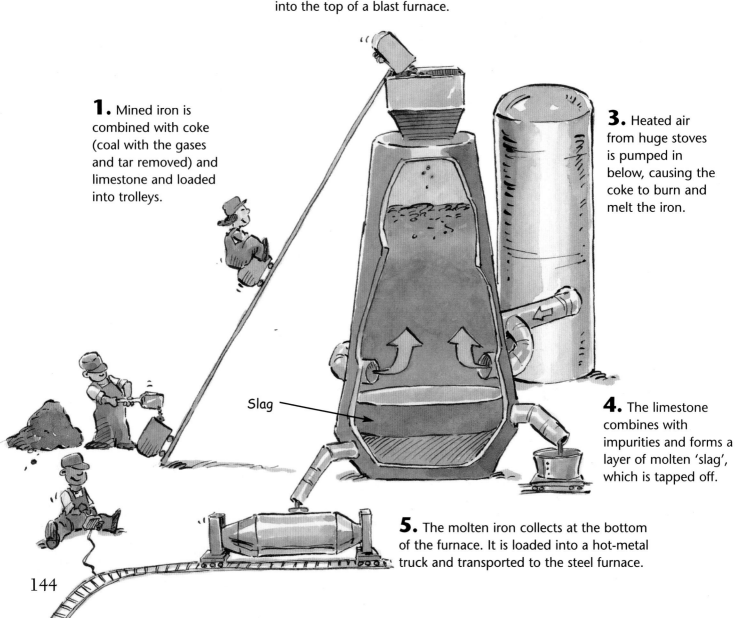

2. The trolleys dump the material into the top of a blast furnace.

1. Mined iron is combined with coke (coal with the gases and tar removed) and limestone and loaded into trolleys.

3. Heated air from huge stoves is pumped in below, causing the coke to burn and melt the iron.

Slag

4. The limestone combines with impurities and forms a layer of molten 'slag', which is tapped off.

5. The molten iron collects at the bottom of the furnace. It is loaded into a hot-metal truck and transported to the steel furnace.

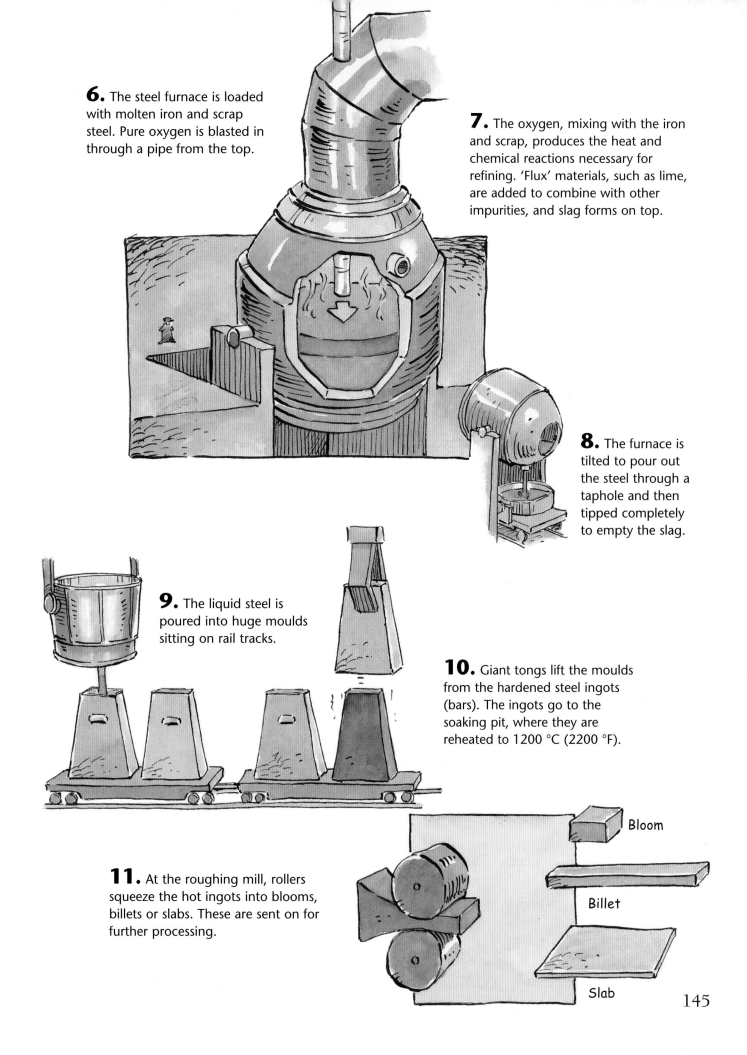

6. The steel furnace is loaded with molten iron and scrap steel. Pure oxygen is blasted in through a pipe from the top.

7. The oxygen, mixing with the iron and scrap, produces the heat and chemical reactions necessary for refining. 'Flux' materials, such as lime, are added to combine with other impurities, and slag forms on top.

8. The furnace is tilted to pour out the steel through a taphole and then tipped completely to empty the slag.

9. The liquid steel is poured into huge moulds sitting on rail tracks.

10. Giant tongs lift the moulds from the hardened steel ingots (bars). The ingots go to the soaking pit, where they are reheated to 1200 °C (2200 °F).

11. At the roughing mill, rollers squeeze the hot ingots into blooms, billets or slabs. These are sent on for further processing.

Bloom

Billet

Slab

145

Timber

1. Woodland trees are selected for their health, straightness and maturity and are cut down with chainsaws. The branches are removed, and the tree is cut into logs for loading onto trucks.

*T*rees are the giants of the plant world in more ways than one. Their leaves absorb carbon dioxide (which is deadly to animals) and release the fresh oxygen we need to live. Their shade keeps us cool on hot summer days, and their leaves and flowers decorate our gardens and parks.

When we harvest them, their woody trunks produce the timber used to build our homes, furniture, fences and many other things.

2. At the mill, the logs are soaked in water to soften the bark and then fed through a debarking machine.

4. The saw operator moves the log to a fixed-position vertical bandsaw that cuts the log lengthwise. The log is cut into thick boards.

Debarked dog

3. Large logs are clamped into position on a rail track. Computerized tools measure each log and calculate how to cut it with the least amount of waste.

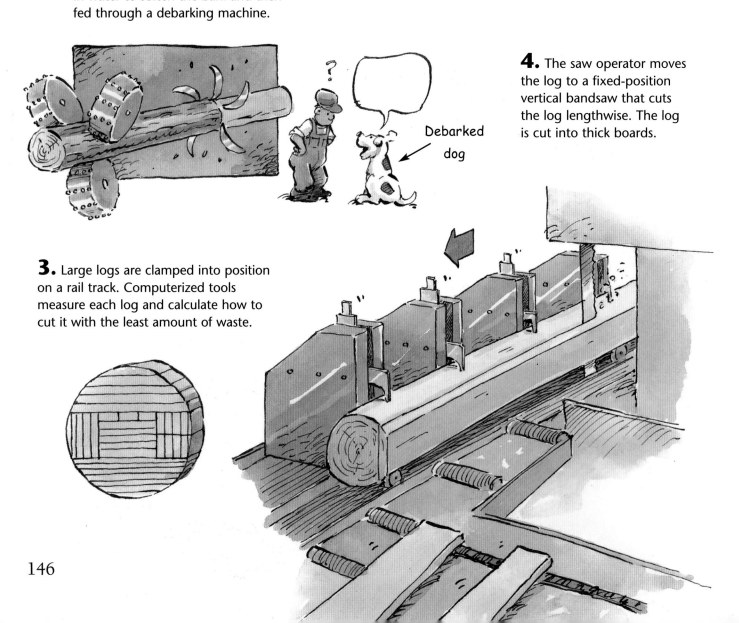

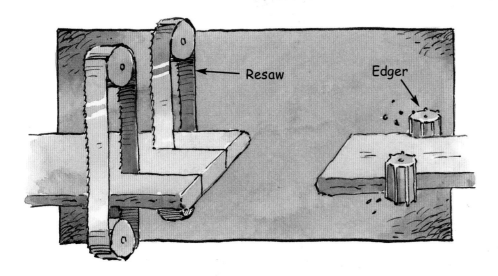

5. The boards then go to the resaw, where bandsaws cut each board to a standard width. Side edgers square the sides of the boards.

6. Smaller logs are sent through a machine called a chipper-canter. This machine has rotating knives that trim off the sides. A second series of adjustable circular saws cut the log into boards, which are then separated by splitters.

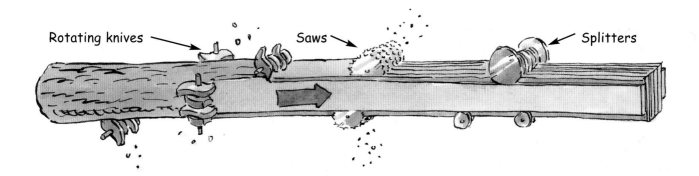

7. Trimmer saws cut the timber to standard lengths, and the timber is graded for size and quality.

8. This 'rough' timber will shrink as it loses moisture, so it is stacked on spacers in a covered, open-air building to dry. For faster drying, timber may be dried in a kiln (oven) in an enclosed building.

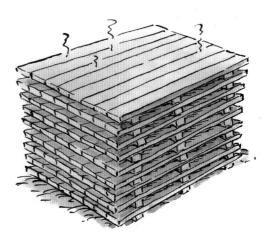

Paper

3. The wood chips are sent to the digester, where chemicals dissolve the lignin (the tree's structural glue), leaving the wood fibres, called pulp. (A lower-quality pulp, used to make newsprint, can be made by mechanically grinding the logs.)

BURRP!

We draw on it, write on it, use it in the bathroom, and decorate our walls with it. We fold it, glue it, bind it, and make toy aeroplanes out of it. We used to think that computers would put an end to it, but the opposite has happened. Today, mainly because of computer needs, we are using more paper than ever.

Where does it all come from? Tear a piece of paper and notice the tiny, hairlike fibres along the tear. That's cellulose, the fibres from the cell walls of trees. It takes a whole lot of trees to make paper. Here's how it's done.

1. Logs arrive at the paper mill and are rolled about in a drum to knock off the bark.

PAPER FROM RAGS

The oldest paper we have examples of was handmade from linen or cotton rags in about AD 150 in China. Rag paper is very strong and long-lasting because of its low acid content.

2. The logs go to a chipper, where rotating knives slice them into tiny bits.

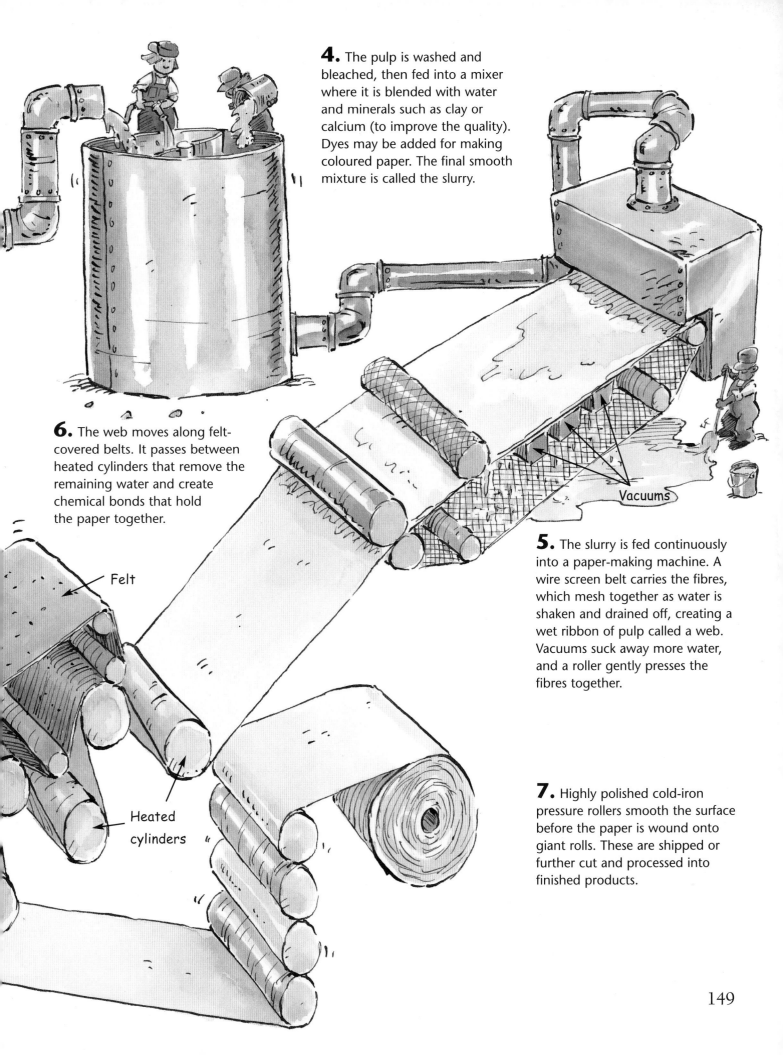

4. The pulp is washed and bleached, then fed into a mixer where it is blended with water and minerals such as clay or calcium (to improve the quality). Dyes may be added for making coloured paper. The final smooth mixture is called the slurry.

6. The web moves along felt-covered belts. It passes between heated cylinders that remove the remaining water and create chemical bonds that hold the paper together.

Vacuums

Felt

Heated cylinders

5. The slurry is fed continuously into a paper-making machine. A wire screen belt carries the fibres, which mesh together as water is shaken and drained off, creating a wet ribbon of pulp called a web. Vacuums suck away more water, and a roller gently presses the fibres together.

7. Highly polished cold-iron pressure rollers smooth the surface before the paper is wound onto giant rolls. These are shipped or further cut and processed into finished products.

Oil

What does your family use to heat your home or power your car? Did you know that even your clothes and toys may have started out as black gooey stuff pumped from the ground?

Derived from a Greek word meaning 'rock' and a Latin word meaning 'oil', petroleum – the proper name for crude oil – was first found seeping from the ground and was not thought to be especially useful. Today, oil is probably the most valuable resource in the world. Although most crude oil is converted into petrol, it is also the basis for a whole range of products, from plastics to candle wax.

1. About 300 million years ago, tiny plants and animals in shallow oceans died, sank and settled at the bottom. They piled up, having no oxygen to break them down.

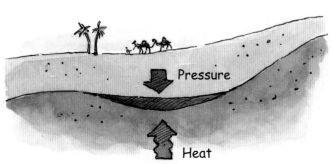

2. Over the years, this mass became buried under sand and sediment and then was pressed and heated by the Earth until it changed into natural gas and black, sticky oil.

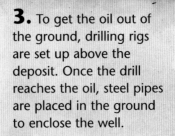

3. To get the oil out of the ground, drilling rigs are set up above the deposit. Once the drill reaches the oil, steel pipes are placed in the ground to enclose the well.

4. At first, the pressure of the gas in the deposit forces the oil to the surface. Over time, a surface rocking arm needs to be installed to pump the oil to the surface.

5. Gas separators and settling tanks remove water, sand, natural gas and other unwanted materials from the crude oil before it is shipped off by pipeline to the refinery.

6. At the refinery, the separated oil is heated, then pumped into a stainless-steel 'fractioning tower'. The oil vapour rises up the tower. Different products (fractions) of the oil vapour condense (become liquid) at different places in the tower.

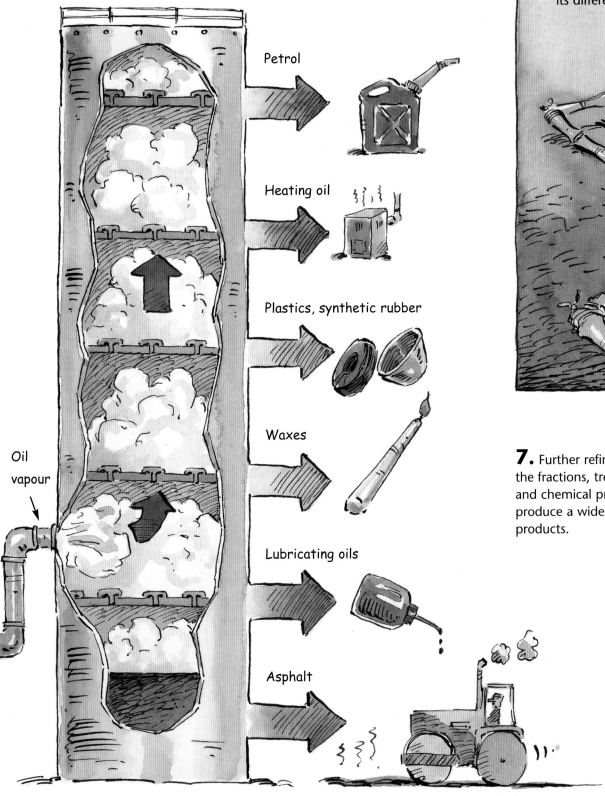

Petrol

Heating oil

Plastics, synthetic rubber

Waxes

Oil vapour

Lubricating oils

Asphalt

7. Further refining of the fractions, treatments and chemical processing produce a wide range of products.

151

Plastic Resins

We live in a world of plastic. It's used to make everything from car bodies and engine parts to toys, bus seats and buttons. Besides thousands of plastic products, there are many different kinds of plastic.

One kind is polythene (polyethylene), used in hundreds of products we see every day, such as squeezy bottles, toys and dustbins. They all begin as plastic pellets of resin, and the pellets start out as ...

1. Plastic begins as oil. At the refinery, the oil is separated into its various parts (including naphtha) using a 'fractioning tower' (*see* Oil, page 150).

4. The mixture is heated under pressure in a polymerization reactor. The ethylene molecules react (change) by linking together into long chains called polymers. These settle to the bottom of the tank in a thick 'slurry'. Each polyethylene chain has more than 1000 ethylene molecules in it.

CHAIN GANG

The linking of small molecules (monomers) into chains (polymers) is what gives different plastics their unique qualities, such as stretchiness, bounce and strength.

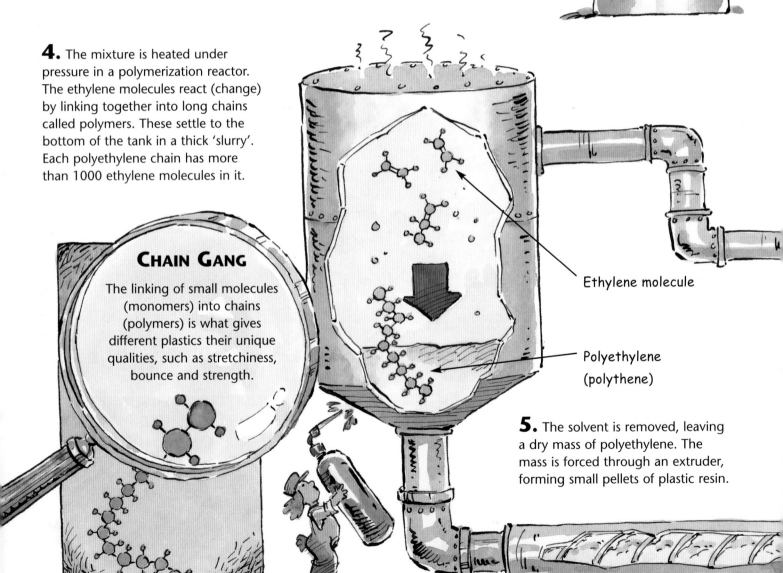

Ethylene molecule

Polyethylene (polythene)

5. The solvent is removed, leaving a dry mass of polyethylene. The mass is forced through an extruder, forming small pellets of plastic resin.

152

2. Naphtha gas is mixed with steam, heated to a high temperature, and then rapidly cooled to create ethylene. This process is called cracking.

Ethylene

3. The ethylene is mixed in a tank with a solvent and a catalyst (a chemical needed to bring about a chemical reaction).

6. The pellets are bagged and shipped off to a plastic-moulding factory.

PELLETS INTO PRODUCTS

Here are five ways to make plastic products out of resin pellets.

Injection moulding: The resin is forced under pressure into a mould. When the plastic hardens, the mould is opened and prepared for the next injection. This is the most common method.

Casting: The melted resin is simply poured into a mould, producing a solid plastic object.

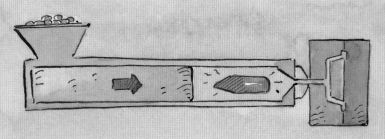

Blow moulding: A tube of resin is placed in a mould. A blast of air or steam blows the resin out to the sides of the mould until it hardens.

Compression moulding: Heat and pressure are applied to a mould containing the plastic resin. Products made this way (called thermoset plastics) include pot handles and engine parts.

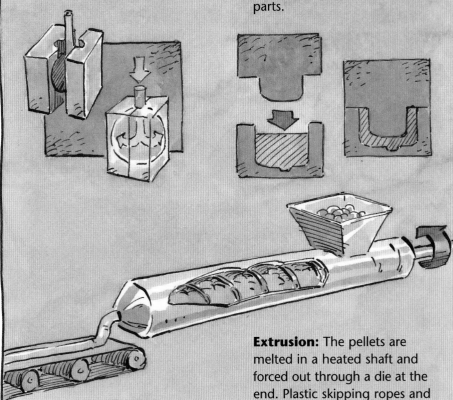

Extrusion: The pellets are melted in a heated shaft and forced out through a die at the end. Plastic skipping ropes and garden hoses are made this way.

153

Recycling

For most of human history, we didn't have recycling as we think of it today. Much of what we used broke down organically and returned to the soil. Other items were burned, and the little that was left over was simply buried.

But as populations grow and the Earth's resources are used up, landfills and incinerators are no longer the only answer. Recycling paper, plastics, glass and metals conserves energy and reduces the pollution released into soil, water and air. And it also saves the Earth's dwindling resources for tomorrow.

Today we sort our rubbish at home, place it in bins for collection, and watch the refuse collectors carry it away. But how many of us really know what happens to it then?

CONSERVATION SCORECARD

✔ Making aluminium from recycled products uses 96 percent less energy than making it from bauxite.

✔ Producing steel from scrap requires 75 percent less energy.

✔ Recycling paper uses 20 percent less energy than making it from raw fibres.

✔ Recycled glass takes 30 percent less energy to produce.

✔ It can take as much or more energy to recycle plastics, but burying them in a landfill creates real problems for the environment, since most plastics do not biodegrade.

1. The refuse collector places paper and cardboard in one bin on the truck, and glass, metals and plastics in another. At sorting plants, the two bins are dumped in two different areas.

Paper

Plastic, metal and glass

7. The flakes are cleaned, dried, melted, and extruded to form small pellets. These can now be sold to plastic factories to make new products, such as recycling bins!

6. Plastics (*see* Plastic Resins, page 152) are divided into groups according to type of plastic, then compacted and baled. At the plastic recycling plant, they are shredded into plastic flakes.

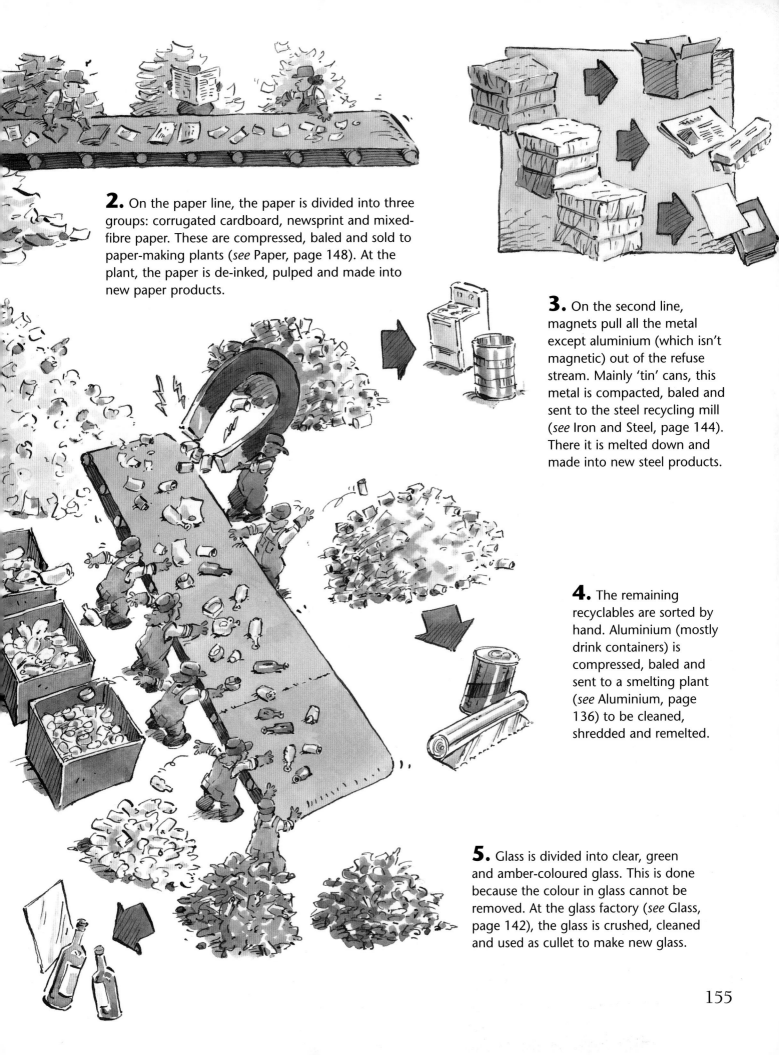

2. On the paper line, the paper is divided into three groups: corrugated cardboard, newsprint and mixed-fibre paper. These are compressed, baled and sold to paper-making plants (*see* Paper, page 148). At the plant, the paper is de-inked, pulped and made into new paper products.

3. On the second line, magnets pull all the metal except aluminium (which isn't magnetic) out of the refuse stream. Mainly 'tin' cans, this metal is compacted, baled and sent to the steel recycling mill (*see* Iron and Steel, page 144). There it is melted down and made into new steel products.

4. The remaining recyclables are sorted by hand. Aluminium (mostly drink containers) is compressed, baled and sent to a smelting plant (*see* Aluminium, page 136) to be cleaned, shredded and remelted.

5. Glass is divided into clear, green and amber-coloured glass. This is done because the colour in glass cannot be removed. At the glass factory (*see* Glass, page 142), the glass is crushed, cleaned and used as cullet to make new glass.

Rubber

What can resist huge bursts of electricity? Keep oceans of water at bay? Leap tall buildings in a single bounce?

Bouncy, stretchy, waterproof rubber!

Europeans first encountered rubber in the New World. There they found the native people of Central and South America using hard rubber balls in their games and spreading latex (the milky white juice of the rubber tree) on their feet to make rubber shoes. The newcomers certainly had nothing like this back home.

The South American native people called the rubber tree *cahuchu*, which means 'weeping wood', because the large white drops of latex that oozed from the tree reminded them of tears.

Today rubber is used in thousands of products, some of which you will read about in this book.

1. It all starts with the rubber tree. Rubber tappers cut a groove in the bark. Latex oozes from the groove into a cup and is collected about every three hours.

2. The latex is poured into a large tank, where it is mixed with the same amount of water and strained to remove bits of bark and twigs.

3. Formic acid is added to make the diluted latex mixture coagulate (thicken into solid particles). The solid rubber particles rise to the top and form a thick, doughy, white lump of crude rubber.

4. The rubber lumps are passed through rollers, which press out the excess water and flatten the rubber into sheets.

5. The sheets of rubber are hung to dry in a smokehouse for a number of days before being baled and shipped off to make tyres and shoes and foam rubber and toys and water bottles and hoses and paints and balls and ...

BUT NOW ...

At least, that's how rubber used to be made. Today, two-thirds of the world's rubber is produced synthetically, in factories. These synthetic rubbers were first developed in the two world wars, when manufacturers were cut off from their sources of natural rubber. Some artificial rubbers are used as replacements for natural rubber; others have been developed for new products, from mattresses to jet aeroplane parts.

Most artificial rubber comes from two products (*see* Oil, page 150), butadiene and sytrene. At the factory, they are combined and mixed with a catalyst (a substance that speeds up a chemical reaction). Antioxidants (substances that slow down deterioration of the rubber when exposed to air) are added in a second tank, and acid and salts in a third. Here the synthetic rubber coagulates, rising to the surface of the liquid as lumps. Then it's on to steps 4 and 5 above.

FIRE AND BRIMSTONE

Early rubber was sticky when hot, and hard and brittle when cold. In 1839, American Charles Goodyear accidentally spilled a rubber-sulphur mixture on the stove and discovered a process called vulcanization, named after the Roman god of fire, Vulcan. Mixing and heating the rubber with sulphur makes the rubber tough yet pliable, no matter what the temperature.

Glossary

alloy
A metal produced by mixing metals and sometimes other substances. For example, steel is an alloy of iron, carbon (a non-metal), and metals such as nickel and manganese.

atom
The smallest particle of matter.

bacteria
Tiny organisms usually made up of a single cell. They are so small you need a microscope to see them.

cell
The smallest part of an organism that can function by itself. Cells can do things such as heal themselves and make new cells. Each cell is enclosed by a membrane which separates it from other cells.

cellulose
The main material in plant-cell walls. Cellulose is used to make paper, rayon and other products.

chemical reaction
A change in the chemical structure of a substance to form another substance. One example is digestion. Your body changes the food you eat into simpler products it uses for energy and repair.

condense
To change from a gas to a liquid or solid form. For example, on a hot day, water vapour (a gas) in the air changes to water (a liquid) when it hits a cold glass of lemonade. In winter, water vapour condenses to ice (a solid) on a cold windscreen.

die
A device for stamping, cutting or moulding material into particular shapes. Some dies are hollow nozzles that form shapes by having materials such as melted plastic forced through them. *See also* extrusion.

dissolve
To become liquid, especially by being placed in a liquid 'solvent' such as water. For example, sugar stirred into hot water dissolves into a sugar solution.

electrolysis
The passing of electricity through a special liquid (called an electrolyte) to bring about a chemical change.

enzyme
Any of various protein substances produced by living cells to help animals and plants live, change and grow.

extrusion
A method of forcing materials such as liquid plastic or metal through a die. Squeezing a ribbon of toothpaste out of a tube is a simple form of extrusion.

fermentation
The breakdown of organic substances into simpler substances. Wine is produced when yeast breaks down the sugar in grape juice into carbon dioxide gas and alcohol.

ingot
A piece of metal that has been formed in a mould. Ingots are suitable for storage and handling.

kiln
A large oven for drying, burning or baking products such as bricks or clay pots.

lubricant
Any oily or slippery substance applied to surfaces to make them rub together more smoothly.

molecule
A group of atoms. The salt molecule, for example, is made up of one atom of sodium and one atom of chlorine.

organism
An individual plant or animal.

pasteurization
A heat treatment for milk, cheese and other foods to destroy harmful organisms.

process
A method of doing or producing something by following a series of planned steps. For example, extrusion is a common manufacturing process.

slurry
A thick mixture of solid particles in a liquid such as water.

synthetic
Made artificially by chemical means. Synthetic materials, such as plastics, do not exist in nature.

vacuum
An empty, airless container or space.

For More Information

Books and Encyclopedias

How It Works: The New Illustrated Science and Invention Encyclopedia (Westport, Conn.: H. S. Stuttman, 1993).

How Products Are Made: An Illustrated Guide to Product Manufacturing (Detroit: Gale Research, 1994).

How Things Are Made, by Felicity Brooks (London: Usborne Publishing, 1989).

How Things Are Made, by Sharon Rose and Neil Schlager (New York: Black Dog and Leventhal, 2003).

How Things Are Made (Washington, D.C.: National Geographic Society, 1981).

The World Book Encyclopedia (Chicago: World Book Inc., 2001).

Web sites

Web sites also provide good information on almost any product you can think of. Use a search engine to find them.

Acknowledgments

In creating a book of this scope, I relied on the skills and expertise of a great many people. The project was moved forward in its early stages through the hard work and research of Sue Dyment, who provided me with much of my information, and Jim Slavin, who wrote most of the original manuscript. I also would like to acknowledge Val Wyatt, the instigator and original editor of this project. Kathy Vanderlinden took over the editor's reins early on and worked with both Jim and me to guide the project through to completion. And last but not least, I'd like to thank my partner, Esperança Melo, who designed the interior pages and calmly and with good humour incorporated my changes on the fly.

Many other individuals and companies helped me with the technical aspects of the writing, but I especially want to thank Don Maynard and Dean Spence, both of whom have a much better mind for this sort of thing than I will ever have, and took the time to answer my many questions.

Index